W9-BYU-512

Saint Peter's University Library
Withdrawn

Terence Rattigan

Twayne's English Authors Series

Kinley E. Roby, Editor
Northeastern University

TEAS 366

TERENCE RATTIGAN
(1911–1977)
Photograph courtesy of Dr. Jan Van Loewen Ltd.

Terence Rattigan

By Susan Rusinko

Bloomsburg State College

Twayne Publishers • *Boston*

Terence Rattigan

Susan Rusinko

Copyright © 1983 by G.K. Hall & Company
All Rights Reserved
Published by Twayne Publishers
A Division of G. K. Hall & Company
70 Lincoln Street
Boston, Massachusetts 02111

Book Production by Marne B. Sultz

Book Design by Barbara Anderson

Printed on permanent/durable acid-free
paper and bound in the United States of
America.

**Library of Congress Cataloging in
Publication Data**

Rusinko, Susan.
Terence Rattigan.

(Twayne's English authors series ;
TEAS 366)
Bibliography: p. 162
Includes index.
1. Rattigan, Terence, Sir—
Criticism and interpretation.
I. Title. II. Series.
PR6035.A75Z85   1983   882'.912
83-271
ISBN 0-8057-6852-1

PR
6035
.A75
Z85
1983

To
My Mother and Father

Contents

About the Author

A native of Pennsylvania, Susan Rusinko earned the Ph.D. in English from the Pennsylvania State University. Her dissertation subject was the language of Harold Pinter's poems and plays. Currently Professor of English at Bloomsburg State College in Pennsylvania, she has reviewed books on modern British drama for *Modern Drama, Shaw Review,* and *World Literature Today.* Other publications include articles on Terence Rattigan and Benn Wolfe Levy for the *Modern British Drama* volumes of the *Dictionary of Literary Biography* (1982), and another on James Bridie for the forthcoming *Critical Surveys* has been accepted. Her interest in modern British drama takes her on frequent trips to London, where she conducts biennial theater study trips in conjunction with her teaching duties.

Preface

Writing as his talent directed him, Sir Terence Mervyn Rattigan wrote his first professionally produced play, *First Episode* (1934), while still an undergraduate at Trinity College, Oxford. By the time of his last play, *Cause Célèbre* (1977), produced while he lay dying of cancer, his achievement included twenty-four stage dramas and more than thirty filmscripts, radio plays, and television scripts. Over the forty-odd years of his career (fifty, if one includes juvenilia), he did not swerve from his intention to write plays. Described by Harold Hobson as the greatest natural talent of any English dramatist of the twentieth century,[1] Rattigan found himself, during a phenomenally successful career, grouped with the fashionable, traditional playwrights of his time. Criticized for not being socially committed, like Shaw, Brecht, and Osborne, Rattigan chose to invest his characters with commitments to themselves and the humanistic values of the prevailing societal structure. Theirs, indeed, are the minuscule triumphs of the average person realized in the midst of loneliness, frustration, and the pain of failure. Consequently, their deeply human and psychologically complex needs are those with which the casual playgoer identifies emotionally and the more sophisticated audience understands.

Now that audiences have absorbed the changes and the new freedoms of the 1956 English stage revolution, they are asking once more for plays with stories that entertain and that move to laughter and to tears, rather than mystify or make angry. Sentiment no longer seems old-fashioned, and the traditional lineaments of a play—a logically developed plot with a story, human conflicts and moral dimensions, a comprehensible purpose, emotional impact, and, above all, life affirmation without distracting aspirations to philosophical complexities or stylistic experimentation—are again asserting themselves. The angry or socially significant plays and the proliferations of Godot's ghosts with their academically heralded cosmic significances have been integrated into dramatic history and occupy an innovative, albeit elitist, place in that history. But the price paid by the new dramatists was the loss of a close relationship between them and audiences which earlier dramatists enjoyed. Among the latter was Rattigan who not only survived two decades of the new waves of drama but returned with some success to the London stage during the 1970s.

In a recent interview, Tom Stoppard commented: "It's interesting, isn't it, that right through the revolution, Ibsen and Chekhov never stopped being done, and today, Ken Tynan, high priest of the revolution, who wouldn't permit Rattigan to be done at the National Theatre, is a citizen of Los Angeles, and Rattigan's *Separate Tables* is being revived in London. . . ."[2] Indeed, even as this book goes to press, *Playbill: The Browning Version* and *Harlequinade* is enjoying critical and popular acclaim at the National's Lyttleton Theatre, with Alec McCowen and Geraldine McEwan in the leading roles. So recognition, always accorded Rattigan by West End audiences, has moved beyond the commercial theaters to small playhouses and even to London's most prestigious theatrical establishment.

A current Rattigan reassessment and renaissance include the publication of the fourth volume of his *Collected Plays* in 1978 and his biography by Michael Darlow and Gillian Hodson in 1979. These were preceded in 1977 by a doctoral dissertation by Holly Hill (the City University of New York) who had worked with Rattigan's papers preceding his death in 1977.

This study is intended only as a beginning assessment of his plays and of his position as dramatic chronicler of the changing moods and attitudes in England through the turbulent middle years of the twentieth century.

For the most part, the plays are discussed chronologically, with particular attention to the increasing openness with which he dealt with contemporary problems in intimately personal experiences of his characters and to his creation of memorable characters that have something in common with those of Osborne, Pinter, and Orton. Stylistically, his adaptation of traditional dramatic techniques, although not revolutionary, is developed as the basis for the unique position that is his. He not only survived stage upheavals during his lifetime but in retrospect can be seen as an important link between the old and the new.

Susan Rusinko

Bloomsburg State College

Acknowledgments

I am indebted to Stanley Weintraub, Anthony Curtis, Michael Darlow, and Holly Hill, whose help from inception to conclusion of this book was inspirational, practical, or both. In particular, I owe much to Michael Darlow for his generosity in allowing me the use of his and Gillian Hodson's biography of Rattigan, to Holly Hill for her graciousness in providing me with her doctoral dissertation—an indispensable source of information and ideas, particularly her perceptive comparison of Rattigan's *The Deep Blue Sea* with Pinero's *Mid-Channel* and generally her lively and keen continuing interest in Rattigan scholarship.

For my earliest encouragement to write, I thank Bloomsburg State College Emeritus Professors Louise and Cecil Seronsy and Emeritus President Harvey A. Andruss. Release time research grants introduced at Bloomsburg by Vice-President for Academic Affairs James Mitchell have contributed much to the completion of the manuscript.

To Geoffrey Davies for guidance through the maze of British theater sources, to the staffs of the Harvey A. Andruss Library and of the British Film Institute, to Joan Walton for her typing help, and to Virginia Duck and Louise Seronsy for invaluable proofreading aid, I am grateful. Special mention must go to those who have been captive audience to problems and progress in the book: Mary Rusinko, Helen and Albert Schutz, Anna and Michael Costa, Virginia Duck, and Mildred Bisgrove.

Source acknowledgments include the following:

The Collected Plays of Terence Rattigan: 1953, Vols. 1 and 2; 1964, Vol. 3; 1978, Vol. 4. London: Hamish Hamilton. By special permission, © Peter F. Carter-Ruck and C. S. Forsyth as Executors and Trustees of the late Sir Terence Rattigan.

Camille and Other Plays. Stephen Stanton, ed. New York: Hill and Wang, 1957.

Dear Me. Peter Ustinov. Boston: Little, Brown and Co., 1977.

Olivier. Logan Gourlay, ed. Briarcliff Manor, N.Y.: Stein and Day, 1974. Reprinted with permission of Stein and Day Publishers.

TERENCE RATTIGAN

"Professional Man and Boy," Anthony Curtis. *Plays and Players,* February 1978, pp. 21–23. By special permission of Anthony Curtis.
The Rise and Fall of the Well Made Play. John Russell Taylor. New York: Hill and Wang, 1967

Chronology

1911	Born 10 June in Kensington, London, to Vera Houston and William Frank Arthur Rattigan.
1920	Enters Mr. W. M. Hornbye's school, Sandroyd.
1925–1930	Attends Harrow on scholarship.
1930–1933	Attends Trinity College, Oxford, where he reads history.
1931–1933	Attends summer foreign-language schools (crammers) in France and Germany.
1933	*First Episode,* with Philip Heimann, opens at Q Theatre near Kew Bridge, 11 September.
1934	*First Episode,* moves to Comedy Theatre, London, 26 January.
1935	*A Tale of Two Cities,* adapted with John Gielgud; remains unproduced until 1950.
1936	*French Without Tears,* 6 November at the Criterion Theatre.
1938	*Follow My Leader,* with Anthony Maurice, banned by Lord Chamberlain.
1939	*After the Dance,* 21 June at St. James Theatre; film of *French Without Tears.*
1939–1945	Serves six years during World War II in the R.A.F.
1940	*Follow My Leader,* 17 January at Apollo Theatre. *Grey Farm* with Hector Bolitho, 3 May at Hudson Theatre, New York; *Quiet Wedding,* film of Esther McCracken's play, with Anatole de Grunwald.
1942	*The Day Will Dawn,* with Anatole de Grunwald from story by Frank Owen; *Flare Path,* 13 August at Apollo Theatre; *Uncensored,* film with Wolfgang Wilhelm and Rodney Ackland.

1943   *While the Sun Shines,* 24 December at the Globe Theatre.

1944   *Love in Idleness,* 20 December at Globe Theatre; *English Without Tears,* a film.

1945   *The Way to the Stars* and *Journey Together,* films about World War II.

1946   *The Winslow Boy,* 23 May at the Lyric Theatre. Wins Ellen Terry award.

1947   Film of *While the Sun Shines; Brighton Rock,* film with Graham Greene.

1948   New York Drama Critics' Award for *The Winslow Boy;* film of *The Winslow Boy,* with Anatole de Grunwald; *Playbill,* 8 September at the Phoenix; Wins Ellen Terry award again; *Bond Street,* film with Rodney Ackland and Anatole de Grunwald.

1949   *Adventure Story,* 17 March at the St. James.

1950   *Who Is Sylvia?,* 24 October at the Criterion; begins epistolary debate in the *New Statesman* on "The Play of Ideas."

1951   Film of *The Browning Version* with Anatole de Grunwald and Ian Dalrymple. Wins Cannes award for best screenplay; *The Final Test* on TV, 29 July.

1952   *The Deep Blue Sea,* 6 March at the Duchess; film, *The Sound Barrier.*

1953   *The Sleeping Prince,* 5 November at the Phoenix; film of *The Final Test.*

1954   *Separate Tables,* 22 September at the St. James; *The Man Who Loved Redheads,* a film.

1955   Film, *The Deep Blue Sea.*

1956   *Separate Tables* repeats its London success in New York.

1957   *The Prince and the Showgirl,* film.

1958   Awarded C.B.E. Birthday Honors by Queen Elizabeth; *Variation on a Theme,* 8 May at the Globe.

1961   BBC television production of *Adventure Story.*

1962   BBC television play, *Heart to Heart,* 6 December.

1963   *The V.I.P.s,* a film; *Man and Boy,* 4 September at the Queen's; *The Girl Who Came to Supper,* 8 December in New York, by Noel Coward. *Ninety Years On* with Noel Coward, BBC tribute to Churchill, 29 November.

1965   *The Yellow Rolls-Royce,* a film.

1966   *Nelson—A Portrait in Miniature,* 21 March on ATV.

1968   In Pompeii for musical remake of *Goodbye Mr. Chips; All on Her Own,* BBC 2, 25 September.

1970   *A Bequest to the Nation,* 23 September at the Theatre Royal.

1971   Knighthood awarded in June.

1973   Film of *A Bequest to the Nation; In Praise of Love* at the Duchess, 27 September.

1974   *Nijinsky,* unproduced television play.

1975   Bone cancer diagnosed during Christmas season; *Cause Célèbre,* radio play aired on BBC 4 on 27 October.

1976   Continues to write in Bermuda, returning to London for treatments. BBC 3 radio interview with Anthony Curtis, 30 March.

1977   *Cause Célèbre,* 4 July at the Haymarket. Undergoes radical operation in May and dies 30 November.

1978   Memorial service at St. Martin's-in-the-Fields, with Donald Sinden reading speech prepared by William Douglas Home, 9 May.

Chapter One

Biography

Unlike many writers whose careers grew out of other professional pursuits or those dramatists whose writing included poetry and fiction, Sir Terence Mervyn Rattigan knew from his earliest schooldays at Harrow that he loved the theater. He also knew that he was not cut out to be an actor, but that indeed he would like someday to be a "famous playwrite." George Bernard Shaw's early interest was music criticism; later he wrote dramatic criticism and still later wrote fiction, along with drama. Somerset Maugham gave up playwriting completely in order to write fiction. Rattigan's interests, however, were single-mindedly dramatic, over a long playwriting career that began in his very early twenties while he was an undergraduate at Oxford in the early 1930s and that continued until his death in 1977. His fascination with the theater was obsessive. Through the five middle decades of the twentieth century, he drew on life as he observed it at Harrow and Oxford, through World War II years as an airman, and then through the turbulent dramatic revolution that occurred in England in the 1950s when his dramatic writing was at its zenith. Withdrawing from the stage in 1963 after the production of *Man and Boy,* he turned to films and to a brief stay in Hollywood, but then returned to the London stage in the early 1970s, writing three more stage plays before his death in 1977. The stage was his life.

Family

Rattigan was born in Kensington, London, on 10 June 1911, to William Frank (C.M.G.) and Vera Houston Rattigan, ten days before the coronation of George V. In later years he frequently referred to the event of his birth which kept his mother from attending the coronation events of 1911.

His father, the son of Sir William Rattigan, K.C., M.P., educated at Harrow and then at Magdalen College, Oxford, was a career diplomat. In

1903 he served in Vienna as attaché and then was appointed Third Secretary in 1905 and Second Secretary in 1909. Active service in World War I interrupted his diplomatic career for several years, but in a resumption of this career in 1916 he was appointed First Secretary. Succeeding postwar appointments included a time as Chargé d'Affaires in Rumania and then in 1921 as Assistant High Commissioner in Constantinople and, subsequently, Acting High Commissioner.

After his resignation from the Foreign Service in 1922, Frank Rattigan published a book, *Diversions of a Diplomat*. He spent his retirement collecting and selling antiques. His collection of English furniture of the seventeenth and eighteenth centuries was sold at auction in New York in 1929 at the Anderson Galleries, who published a book on the collection ("Queen Anne, Chippendale, Sheraton and earlier English furniture; paintings, ceramics, bibelots").[1]

Both of Rattigan's grandfathers were barristers, and so it is not mere chance that famous English court trials as well as diplomats, foreigners, and historical events play such a large part in the subject matter of his drama.

School Years

Like his father, Terence attended Harrow and then Oxford, but his college was Trinity, not Magdalen. Tradition ran deep in Rattigan's life, and he read history at Oxford, his family intending him to follow in his father's diplomatic footsteps and traditionally privileged life.

At Harrow, however, which Rattigan attended on scholarship, he discovered Galsworthy, Chekhov, and Shaw. In fulfillment of a French assignment, he wrote a short play about Cesar Borgia, for which he received his first review from a master who proclaimed his French to be execrable but his sense of theater first class, a sense which was to distinguish a long dramatic career. In his Harrow days he also played a brief role in a one-act play. "During rehearsals he let work slip, and the headmaster offered him a choice between abandoning the part and taking a beating. He chose the beating."[2]

His solid English background also included participation in cricket at Harrow, another lifelong interest that would become a subject for a play. "I used to stonewall at one end . . . while the other chap lashed out."[3] He later wrote about "lying on his hard school bed, his soul split between the rival dreams of making witty first-night speeches to wildly cheering houses (after being kissed by Marie Tempest and Gladys Cooper simultaneously) and of bowling out the entire Australian eleven for thirteen (eight of which I usually conceded to my hero, Macartney, the rest being byes)."[4] His 1951 television play, *The Final Test,* was an inevitable outgrowth of that early Harrovian division of time between theater and cricket.

As early as his eleventh year, then, Rattigan became a "confirmed and resolute playgoer."[5] He dreamed of having his works "described as being by 'the famous playwrite and author, T. M. Rattigan.'"[6] Among his earliest writing efforts, according to Rattigan, "there is only one example of non-dramatic fiction extant, a piece of early prep school vintage, entitled 'Self-Sacrifice,' 'an enthralling novelette by that famous—etc.' and abandoned halfway down page three. But even on this title page the word 'playwrite' took precedence over mere 'author', and it is very plain in which direction my main ambitions lay."[7] Meantime, Rattigan wrote,

Up in the galleries (or, as my pocket money increased proportionately with my snobbishness, down in my pits), I was experiencing emotions which, though no doubt insincere of origin in that they were induced and coloured by the adult emotions around me, were none the less most deeply felt.

When I came, therefore, to try to reproduce, as a precocious playwright, the emotions that had been aroused in myself as a precocious member of an audience, the results, though no doubt ludicrous, were at least instinctively theatrical. It was by no cold and conscious exercise that I was able to act as audience to my own plays. I could not have written them otherwise. Aunt Edna, [Rattigan's fictional audience—middle class England] in fact, or at least her juvenile counterpart, was inside my creative brain and in pleasing her I was only pleasing myself.[8]

His attendance at theaters as a very young boy gradually developed into an obsession that was to determine the course of his life and the inevitable clash with his father. Parental plans for a diplomatic career were destined for rejection in that earliest dramatic attempt at Harrow, "Cesar Borgia."

At Oxford Rattigan's interest in theater developed further as a result of his serving as dramatic critic of the *Cherwell,* the undergraduate paper.

When I was at Oxford I was dramatic critic of the *Cherwell,* the undergraduate paper. I used to go religiously to the Oxford Repertory Theatre, every Monday night and the performance was always terrible because, poor loves, they could never get it right. I was continually after them for not getting their lines right or the Duke was wearing threadbare trousers—you know, really cheeky, bad undergraduate criticism. Then after a time when I'd written several plays— none of which had been performed—I wrote to St. John Ervine, asking him whether I should chuck it and become a drama critic. He answered, roughly, "Don't. Press on. I haven't read any of your plays and I'm sure they're pretty awful, but it's better to be a creative writer than a critic."[9]

At Oxford Rattigan also tried his hand at acting in a production of *Romeo and Juliet* (with Edith Evans, directed by John Gielgud) in a one-line role as halberdier. "Terence Rattigan had a single line to speak as one of the musicians who came to awaken Juliet for her wedding, a traumatic experience for him, one gathers, which in later years he was to make use of, for he built his one-act comedy, *Harlequinade,* around a touring company's production of *Romeo and Juliet* in which his solitary 'put up your pipes' line was featured."[10]

An amusing comedy, *Harlequinade* is about provincial actors rehearsing *Romeo and Juliet.* Offstage and onstage events confusingly crisscross, and older and younger members of the acting profession during the rehearsal comment on the state of the contemporary stage in England. Causing even more, if rather minor, problems is the actor playing the halberdier, who runs in, frequently on miscue, to recite his one line, the one Rattigan had so much difficulty with at Oxford: "Faith, we may put up our pipes and begone."

Referring to his brief acting experience in an interview with Philip Oakes in 1976, Rattigan "realized very early that I was not cut out to be an actor. . . . And I was in an OUDS production of 'Romeo and Juliet' with Edith Evans and Peggy Ashcroft and Johnny Gielgud directing. I wore the baggiest of tights and an awful wig and everyone howled with laughter. Gielgud coached me and coached me but although I had only one line I kept fluffing it. He was in absolute despair."[11]

From his earliest years Rattigan as playwright, actor, critic drew on his background and the life he knew for his plays. Undergraduate life became the subject for his first produced play, a collaboration with Philip Heimann, *First Episode* (1934), while his first huge success, *French Without Tears* (1936), is a sparkling romantic comedy about young prospective diplomats studying French in the home of their instructor on the French Riviera. Another moderately successful play, *After the Dance* (1939), is concerned with two generations, the younger of which is maturing in pre–World War II London and the older, which grew up at the close of World War I. The first takes itself most seriously in attempts to reform the aimless, disillusioned life patterns of the older group with results that are destructive even as they serve as catalysts for change. It is a gray prewar world indeed, especially as contrasted with the exuberance and carefree existence of the French-language students in *French Without Tears*. The moods of Rattigan's plays vividly reflect those of the era and in most cases the moods of Rattigan's own personal life. *Follow My Leader* (a 1938 farce produced in 1940), a satire on Hitler, was banned in early production attempts. Like *Grey Farm* (1940) it was a collaboration, the former with Anthony Maurice and the latter with Hector Bolitho.

Professional Dramatist

By now Rattigan had settled in London, having successfully opposed his father's choice of a diplomatic career and then having persuaded his parents to finance him in a dramatist's career. However, World War II temporarily interrupted his desire to write more plays and to prove those critics wrong who referred to the long run of *French Without Tears* as a "lucky fluke" and to himself as "one-play Rattigan."[12] But this "longing had to remain unfulfilled for six long years until, in the intervals of whirling about over the South Atlantic in uneventful search of seemingly non-existent submarines," he wrote *Flare Path,* which "at long last" commended him "if not exactly as a professional playwright, at least as a promising apprentice who had definitely begun to learn the rudiments of his job."[13] Those years of service in the Royal Air Force supplied Rattigan with subject matter for many plays and films of the 1940s. He enjoyed record-breaking successes with *While the Sun Shines* and *Love in Idleness* (American title, *O Mistress Mine*).

In 1940 Rattigan also began his film ventures, writing the script for Esther McCracken's play *Quiet Wedding*. A long film association with Anatole de Grunwald (producer) and Anthony Asquith (director) began with this film, which was followed by a series of World War II films about servicemen and their families: *The Day Will Dawn* (about the German invasion of Norway); *The Way to the Stars,* in America titled *Johnny in the Clouds: Journey Together,* made for the Ministry of Information by the R.A.F. Film Production Unit. Two other films, *Brighton Rock* (about gang warfare) and *Bond Street,* were produced in 1948, preceded the previous year by a film of the play *While the Sun Shines. The Winslow Boy* (1946), about a famous English court trial, and the twin bill of *The Browning Version* and *Harlequinade* (1948) climaxed a highly productive decade of writing for the stage and film, marked by two Ellen Terry Awards for *The Winslow Boy* and *The Browning Version*.

At the end of this ten-year period, Rattigan ventured into his first dramatic treatment of a historical character, Alexander, in *Adventure Story* (1949). He regarded the play as a test and reacted to its mixed reception by the critics as follows: "Actors and writers both have their testing times. For actors it's daring to play big classical roles. They have to take the chance if they want to be really judged. For me the test was to write 'Adventure Story,' my play about Alexander the Great. And now I'm bound to acknowledge that it didn't work. I wasn't ready." He went on to comment about a desire to "re-write chunks of it. . . ."[14]

A Major Playwright

But if the 1930s and 1940s were a time of impressive Shaftesbury runs and a variety of solid dramas and comedies, the 1950s were for Rattigan years of self-confident playwriting which he began by initiating a long debate on the theater in the *New Statesman and Nation.* His attack on the play of ideas was a reaffirmation of his lifelong belief that for him plays are about people, not things. Involved in the debate were the major dramatists of the time, including Christopher Fry, Sean O'Casey, and George Bernard Shaw. The debate provided Rattigan with a forum for a defense of his poesy, although, as the correspondence grew, it developed into an acrimonious debate. Rattigan did have the last word, however, in his concluding article written after Shaw, "the big gun," had finally entered the lists.

In 1953 Rattigan had the satisfaction of having published the first two volumes of his collected plays. One more volume was published in 1964. In all three, he wrote prefaces in which he discussed the progress of his career and continued the defense of his poetics. Volume 4 was not published until a year after his death, and four early plays still remain unpublished.

The 1950s, Rattigan's golden decade, reflected a wide diversity of subject matter, style, and media, including *The Final Test,* a play for television (1951), which was filmed in 1953. But more importantly there was a sharp increase in the highly concentrated tragic-ironic dramas of characters previously handled in a comic or comic-serious style. These include some of his best work, plays that belong to that genre labeled by some critics as the art of humiliation. Of these, *Separate Tables* (1954) is probably his best-known play in America. *The Deep Blue Sea* (1952) and *Variation on a Theme* (1958), also in that genre, along with two fantasies, *The Sleeping Prince* (1953) and *Who Is Sylvia?* (1950), illustrate Rattigan's dramatic versatility.

These stage successes, as well as his television and film work, were mixed with a series of personal events that made this golden time also a sad one. Among these was his father's death in March 1952. In 1953 Rattigan attended with his beautiful mother the gala opening of *The Prince and the Showgirl*, a theatrically royal event in itself, resplendent with the presence of Sir Laurence Olivier and Marilyn Monroe (and Arthur Miller). The stage play on which the film was based was "an occasional fairy tale," honoring both Queen Elizabeth II in her coronation year and Rattigan's mother, to whom he dedicated the play. Royal honors followed in 1958 when he was awarded the C.B.E. at the Queen's Birthday Honors.

Yet with all the public recognition accorded him during this time, Rattigan felt keenly the "old-fashioned" label given him by the critics. So at the age of forty-five he flirted with the idea of moving to Hollywood, but after a six-week stay decided that no long-term contract or any amount of money could convince him to live there.

And for all the fantasy of *The Sleeping Prince,* Rattigan was increasingly dramatizing loneliness and frustration, sexual and social, as in *The Deep Blue Sea, Separate Tables,* and *Variation on a Theme.* All three plays are hard, psychologically realistic portraits of highly sensitive people who have dared to challenge the hypocrisy of prevailing social attitudes toward marital and sexual problems, to confront deeply felt frustrations, and to make choices at the risk of social disapproval. Foreshadowings of these richly drawn mid-century dramatic portraits are to be found in Rattigan's earliest plays, such as *First Episode, After the Dance,* and *Flare Path,* where the problems are either eventually assimilated into conventional patterns of behavior or, as in Chekhov's plays, quietly endured. It is as though in the earlier plays sexual and emotional repressions have little or no opportunity for expression and must bide their time until social attitudes are liberalized. Ironically, the liberalization occurred during the very decade, 1954–1964, when he increasingly felt himself becoming an artistic exile from the English stage.

Also, Rattigan's own homosexuality was never a secret from those who knew him. He neither hid nor flaunted it but remained all his life in a viable social pattern in the worlds of both homosexuality and heterosexuality. Yet he had to dramatize homosexuals as women (*The Deep Blue Sea*) or as women molesters (*Separate Tables*). The disguise for Rattigan was not an evasion, however, as he was more interested in dramatizing deep emotional commitments of characters to a personal honesty and integrity than in exploiting sexual sensationalism. In fact, after he had written the original version of Major Pollock as a homosexual and then changed him to a heterosexual, he tried to go back to the original. However, the "reconception had become so real that it could not be bent back."[15] The basic emotional and moral experience remained intact, regardless of the particular sexual form it took.

The 1950s, a time of economic and personal consolidation after World War II, were for Rattigan a time of disguised attitudes, beneath whose surfaces lay intensely personal pains. His Major Pollock, Sybil Railton-Bell, and Hester Collyer struggled to maintain what personal dignity society would allow them. It is these same frustrations which were to explode with a vengeance in the plays of John Osborne and which were guarded from intruders so zealously in Harold Pinter's plays.

Ironically, Rattigan was at the height of his dramatic success when the stage revolution broke around him. The tabloids were publicizing his personal and professional successes, making of him a "cause célèbre." His position as England's foremost playwright seemed unshakable. Newspaper headlines referred to him as "the golden boy" and "jackpot Rattigan."

At 42, he is handsome, tactfully urbane, and transparently Harrovian; you might imagine him to be an immensely fashionable psychiatrist.

He plays golf regularly at Sunningdale, where his handicap, after repeated protests from the other members has just been reduced from 12 to nine.

He belongs to the Bachelors' Club and the Garrick: what is more (much more), he lives in Eaton Square and has his wallpaper specially designed for him.

He is impenitently prosperous, so much so that the deceptive ease of his success has put many of his critics on the defensive. "Good theatre," they concede, "but. . . ."

In spite of buts, he is the only dramatist in history who has twice achieved a run of 1000 performances. . . . Film scripts from *The Way to the Stars* to *The Final Test* have multiplied his income.[16]

Yet as Rattigan was enjoying his success and even as *Separate Tables* was in its long run on the London stage, John Osborne's angry young man, Jimmy Porter, appeared in *Look Back in Anger,* and suddenly Rattigan felt himself belittled and old-fashioned overnight, as it were. In mellower years, after the new waves of drama had subsided and he was once more a dramatist of critical consequence, particularly to younger critics and audiences, he found himself "in the enviable position of seeing his reputation buoyant once more after years of being consigned to the plushy hinterland of Establishment writers. It's all nonsense, really, he says. 'Critics started to berate me as far back as the 1930's for producing the "well-made play" and I remember writing livid articles for the New York Times defending my position. I feel now as I felt then. I never could see why craftsmanship should be equated with insincerity. I write as well as I can. One should never bore an audience. And it's a bit of a joke to think of the writers whose names were used to belabour me. John Osborne and Harold Pinter for example, Two superb craftsmen, both writers of exceptionally well-made plays. They'd be annoyed if anyone suggested otherwise.'"[17]

To Sheridan Morley, Rattigan talked about his plays "running simultaneously all the way up Shaftesbury Avenue from the Lyric to the Globe. Then, overnight almost, we were told we were old-fashioned and effete and corrupt and finished, and although I was a decade or two younger than Coward or Priestley, I somehow accepted Tynan's verdict and went off to Hollywood to write film scripts."[18] "There I was in 1956, a reasonably successful playwright with *Separate Tables* just opened, and suddenly the whole Royal Court [where *Look Back in Anger* opened] thing exploded, and Coward and Priestley and I were all dismissed, sacked by the critics."[19]

Diversity and a Mellowing

Rattigan wrote three more plays shortly after the Osborne explosion: *Variation on a Theme* (1958), *Ross* (1960), and *Man and Boy* (1963). But in spite of the solidity of their reception and their unusually free treatments of sexual topics, Rattigan's stage playwriting career ended for nearly a decade, as the impact of the new drama sent him into a self-imposed exile of film writing, even a brief stay in Hollywood. So the 1960s were filled with a diversity of film and television activity. A musical adaptation of *French Without Tears* entitled *Joie de Vivre* was produced in 1960, but with no great success. And there were more than minor successes in BBC's televising of *Adventure Story* with Sean Connery (1961) and of *Heart to Heart,* with Ralph Richardson and Kenneth More (1962). The latter is a searing satire on politics and television interviewing.

The year 1963 saw the filming of Rattigan's *The VIPs* and the New York production of Coward's musical adaptation of *The Sleeping Prince,* entitled *The Girl Who Came to Supper.* The film *The Yellow Rolls-Royce* (1965) was released and, like *The VIPs,* featured a star-studded cast and a generally lavish production. Both films reverted to Rattigan's early style of *Flare Path* with the multi-narrative plot in which lives of people from different walks of life crisscrossed by means of some event of the time.

Thus, the 1960s, in spite of the solid film achievements, saw the twilight of Rattigan's long stage career. His disillusionment with Hollywood and film writing was heightened by two sad events. In 1967 Anatole de Grunwald, the friend with whom he had worked so many years, died. A few years later, in 1971, his mother, to whom Rattigan had been devoted and of whom he was so proud during their brief stay in the United States, died. In still another ironic twist of events, Rattigan was made a knight just a few days after his mother's death in 1971. His birth had prevented her attendance at the 1911 coronation events, and now her death had precluded her participation in her son's knighting.

During his short stay in Hollywood Rattigan had lived with the Rex Harrisons while Kay Kendall (Mrs. Harrison) was dying of leukemia. Rattigan himself shortly experienced his first confrontation with death when his own illness was, as it later turned out, wrongfully diagnosed as leukemia. In addition, he suffered a burst appendix while on location in Italy for the musical remake of *Goodbye Mr. Chips.* He talked freely of the unsanitary conditions of the Naples hospital and his second close encounter with death. Of the inaccurately diagnosed leukemia he said, "Either it had mysteriously gone away or the diagnosis had been wrong in the first place. Anyway, I used the experience and put it into a play."[20] The play, of course, is *In Praise of Love.*

Rattigan's residences during his exile from the London stage included Hollywood, Ischia, Paris, and Bermuda. Both health and taxes figured importantly in his decision to establish residency outside England. When he returned to London in 1970 with the stage version of his television play *The Nelson Affair,* retitled *A Bequest to the Nation,* both playwright and play were received warmly. The much-publicized film version of the play appeared in 1973 with Peter Finch and Glenda Jackson in leading roles.

Early in 1976 Rattigan's cancer was discovered, and unlike the earlier diagnosis, this one proved accurate. He spent most of the remaining two years of his life between his home in Bermuda and hospitals in London. In retrospect, the situation of *In Praise of Love,* written between his two illnesses, seems a premonition of real-life events. The play deals with a wife with a terminal illness and the manner in which her son, husband, and friend cope with their knowledge of her condition.

Rattigan's last play, *Cause Célèbre,* opened in London in July 1977. "Somehow, by a supreme effort of will, and with the help of his loyal aide

Peggy French, he managed to rise from his sickbed in the King Edward VII's Hospital for Officers, put on a dinner-jacket and attend the opening night at Her Majesty's. A small crowd gathered outside the stagedoor to cheer him as he left."[21] His final active participation in the theater gracefully suited and completed the pattern of Rattigan's life. That stage curtain about which he had dreamed as a very young boy came down for the last time on a lifelong romance with the theater.

Rattigan died at his Bermuda home on 30 November 1977, still wanting to write a play about former Prime Minister Asquith, father of Anthony Asquith, Rattigan's longtime director-friend. He left unwritten his autobiography, which was to have been titled *Without Tears*. His death occasioned prolific outpourings of appreciation by the young and the old, the avant-gardists and the traditionalists, the theatrically elite and the average theater-goer. They were tributes to everything about Rattigan that was impeccably English and to his sensitive, generous, gentle, warm, humorous humanity. Some of the tributes caught the very substance and style of Rattigan's plays:

Like Terry himself, his plays are not what they seem. With his perfect manners and impeccable dress, his background of Harrow, Oxford, and the RAF, he appeared to be a complete model of the conforming upper-class Englishman just as his works appear to be perfect specimens of the well-made play. In reality he was not in the least conforming and related more to the world of Joe Orton (whose first play he backed) than that of Sir Harold Nicolson. There was a deeply Proustian ambivalence at the heart of him that needs, as they say, to be gone into.[22]

David Rudkin, one of England's important young playwrights, detected "in his plays a deep personal, surely sexual pain, which he manages at the same time to express and disguise. The craftmanship of which we hear so much loose talk seems to me to arise from deep psychological necessity, a drive to organize the energy that arises out of his own pain. Not to batten it down but to invest it with some expressive clarity that speaks immediately to people, yet keeps himself hidden." Rudkin's assessment was aired before Rattigan's death and Rattigan responded by saying that "Rudkin was fascinating . . . He's quite right, of course . . . but I never thought my slip showed as much as that, [nor] if it did, [that] the author of *Afore Night Come* would be the one to spot it."[23]

None of the tributes probably would have pleased Rattigan more than those he received during the last few years of his life, as in a revival of *The*

Browning Version at the King's Head Theatre in 1975 during which he witnessed the "rapt attention given the play by the mass of blue denim that had packed into the pub to see it and the ovation given at the end to Nigel Stock and Barbara Jefford who played the Crock and Millie."[24] It was somehow touchingly appropriate that "those applauding [did not] know that the elderly gentleman in the immaculate dark blue suit at one of the centre tables, dining solely off a wineglass full of Scotch, looking as if it might be Sauterne, was the author."[25]

Rattigan ended his life as he had begun it in those early formative years; only now the dreams of "the curtain rising" had been realized.

Chapter Two
A Sense of Theater

A biographical statement about Rattigan would be incomplete without some comment on his overall dramatic theories—what he called his sense of theater—and on his working habits and long associations with some of the most successful theatrical artists of his time.

Ambivalences: Rattigan's Essence

To begin, the deep ambivalences in Rattigan's personal life are in themselves the essence of dramatic tension and conflict: a homosexual in a rigidly heterosexual society; a son in opposition to a father's will in the matter of a career; inheritance of an idyllically Edwardian tradition in a contemporary world increasingly void of traditional values and verities; the insistence of the importance of the individual within a rigidly structured tradition of social attitudes; deep emotional and physical needs which existing conduct patterns thwart; a tax exile from a country he loved very much; an artistic exile for several years from the London stage, about which he later had pangs of regret.

Above all, he nurtured the writer-audience ambivalence which drove him to a lifelong devotion to everything dramatic. He regarded playwrighting as a "controlled schizophrenia which will allow a dramatist to act as an audience to his own plays while in the very process of writing it."[1] Excited by the magical words "The curtain rises to disclose," he regarded the actual writing process as "an irksome drudgery, inducive of hysteria and destructive of the nerves."[2] This writer-audience ambivalence constituted what he called his sense of theater, a necessary part of which is the consciousness of "being a member of my own audience, and of participating myself in the emotions that I, as author, had aroused in them."[3]

He saw the playwright as an artist uniquely different from the novelist, the music composer, and the painter, for whom that "mysterious sixth sense or split mind" is not there and for whom "talent is all."[4] When, at the age of eleven, the juvenile counterpart of Aunt Edna (his fictional audience) was inside his "creative brain" he felt it so firmly that he wished it "known that the following cast might be suitable for a presentation of this work. . . . Godfrey Tearle, Gladys Cooper, Marie Tempest, Matheson Lang, Isobel Elsom, Henry Ainley—and of a promising young actor over whom I hesitated long before finally giving him the five-line role of a comic poet—Noel Coward."[5]

The audience-half of himself is dominant in Rattigan's early plays as he delighted playgoers for two decades with quintessentially and impeccably upper-middle-class characters and situations. It remained for later plays, beginning with *The Browning Version,* for the submerged half of Rattigan's talent to assert itself with a forcefulness which "serious" audiences and critics applauded.

Rattigan, however, always kept in touch with both muses, even when one seemed to be dominant. As audience, Aunt Edna was never lost sight of. "Write for her and you cannot fail. She will be listened to—she always is; and for those who feel that all the problems of the modern theatre might be solved by her liquidation, let me remind them that she is immortal. . . . Seriously though a playwright must be audience-conscious, not *for* an audience but he must have a split mind and be his own audience. A novelist can lose his reader for a few pages; a playwright never dares lose his audience."[6]

What Theater Is Not

Still, freely as Rattigan spoke about his theater instinct and his talent as gifts about which he never had any doubts, he insisted with equal certainty on the necessity of shaping that talent and "sense of theatre" with the industry and skill of a master craftsman. So, admitting the difficulty of defining "a sense of theatre," he began by stating what it is not.

First and foremost, it has little to do with an ill-made play. For "I believe sloppy construction, untidy technique, and lack of craftsmanship to be grave faults, the more grave in that they may, with nothing more than industrious application, be so easily avoided. I am perfectly prepared to concede that rules are made to be broken, but I think that at least they should be learnt first."[7]

Second, theater sense has nothing to do with eloquence, the poetic gift, or the powers of rhetoric. Rattigan mentioned, in particular, the recent attempted revolution in dramatic language by T. S. Eliot and Christopher

Fry, as well as lesser figures, to rescue "the theatre from the thraldom of middle-class vernacular in which it has been held, with rare intervals, since Tom Robertson. . . ."[8] Rather, as "with Tchekov's Trigorin, . . . everybody must write as he pleases and as best as he may. I 'please to write' in the naturalistic convention and the 'best I may' would quickly become the worst if I denied myself my gift for telling a story and delineating character in the terms of everyday speech."[9] In a series of letters to the *New Statesman and Nation* during an epistolary debate on the play of ideas in 1950, Rattigan was taken to task by several responders for his lack of poetic, imaginative, symbolic, rhetorical, or intellectual language. He continued during his long career to echo the spoken language as he heard it.

A third point in Rattigan's definition of theater sense is closely related to his insistence on the naturalism of spoken dialogue. The "sense of theatre does not lie in the explicit. An analysis of those moments in the great plays at which we have all caught our breaths would surely lead to the conclusion that they are nearly always those moments when the least is being said, and the most suggested. 'As kill a King? . . . Ay Lady 'twas my word.' 'She'll come no more. Never, never, never, never, never.' 'Finish, good lady, the bright day is done and we are for the dark. . . .' 'Mother, give me the sun.' "[10]

What Theater Is

Rattigan's practice of naturalistic and implicit language is vividly illustrated in the final lines of most of his plays. The flat, terse, extraordinarily ordinary language succeeds in evoking complex realities and in giving actors the freedom they need to communicate those realities. Crocker-Harris's "Come along, my dear. We mustn't let our dinner get cold,"[11] after an exhausting day in which the personal and professional humiliations and injuries of a lifetime have been exposed, contains a painful mixture of failure and yet a release that comes with its having been dealt with. In the farewell between Hester Collyer and Freddie Page in *The Deep Blue Sea,* Freddie responds to Hester's intention to go to art school and start from the beginning again. "Good idea. It's never too late to begin again. Isn't that what they say?"[12] Hester "stands by the fire for a moment, watching the flame change from orange to red. She has turned back to the sofa, and is quietly folding one of Freddie's scarves as the curtain falls."[13] Her final spoken word to Freddie is a loud, clear "Goodbye." No amount or kind of literary language could so effectively communicate the dark future of Hester, who has gone beyond despair because she has no hope.

"I am sure that this instinct for the use of dramatic implication is in fact a part of the mystique of playwrighting," wrote Rattigan, "and, in my view, by far the most important part; for it is the very quality that can transform a mere sense of theatre into a sense of drama. I am equally sure that it is, in fact, an instinct, unhappily not to be learnt, but only inherited, in that it implies in its possessor a kind of deformity of the creative mind, a controlled schizophrenia. . . . It is the eccentric faculty, and only this, that will enable him to master those most vital problems of the whole craft of playwriting—what *not* to have your actors say, and how best to have them *not* say it."[14] Rattigan is doing the very thing for which Pinter became so famous, different as the plays of the two dramatists are. It is, moreover, the very quality that has attracted the giant acting talents of Rattigan's time to his plays.

The possibilities for actors, the very best, such as Laurence Olivier and Margaret Leighton, are obvious. Rattigan found that famous players were eager to be cast in his work. His early dream at Harrow of having the best actors in his plays was realized throughout his lifetime. There were the duos of Olivier-Leigh, Olivier-Monroe, Leighton-Portman, Lunt-Fontanne, Burton-Taylor, Finch-Jackson. From his earliest major success, *French Without Tears,* to his last one, *Cause Célèbre,* illustrious names headlined notices and reviews of his dramas: Roland Culver, Rex Harrison, Jessica Tandy, Alfred Lunt, Lynne Fontanne, Peggy Ashcroft, Paul Scofield, Laurence Olivier, Vivien Leigh, Margaret Leighton, Donald Sinden, Glynis Johns, Kenneth More, Alec Guinness, Claire Bloom, Eric Portman, and the list goes on and on.

The Art of the Scene or the Short Play

Rattigan's structural technique, of which he was a master, was that of the short play, a natural consequence of his emphasis on the importance of scene construction. Many of his short plays were written to be performed in tandem: *Playbill,* consisting of *The Browning Version* and *Harlequinade; Separate Tables,* composed of *Table Number Seven* and *Table by the Window; In Praise of Love,* which included *After Lydia* and *Before Dawn.* A *Mutual Pair* was a title considered for one of several versions of his Nelson play. *Adventure Story* is so divided that the second act in its passive contrast with the first was considered by some reviewers to weaken the play. In most of

Rattigan's other plays, such as *First Episode* and *Cause Célèbre,* two or more plots appear at times to vie with each other. The existence of the dual plot or multi-plot, indeed, is a deliberate structural quality, as one story-line supports or provides a context for the other. They are always closely joined at a crucial point in the events by some common bond, and together create a unity and complexity of characterization achieved by Rattigan only by this means.

Rattigan's structure does not follow the prescribed Scribean formula in which withheld secrets and abundant coincidences create tensions and complications which rise to a climax and then fall in patterned fashion to the expected conclusion. Nor is it the structure of Coward, to whom he has so often been likened, for Coward dispenses with plot almost entirely to create characters in situations rather than in plots. And, third, Rattigan's is not the structure of the problem plays of Galsworthy and Pinero, to which *The Winslow Boy* and *The Deep Blue Sea* have frequently been likened. The heavy exposition of their plays are not Rattigan's. Nor are their decisive, frequently suicidal endings those of Rattigan, where the more natural rhythms of life prevail.

The Primacy of People

For Rattigan, the conventional climax and the mechanically contrived ending deflect attention from what is the most important element in his dramas—people. Wherever and whenever conventions are needed for honest delineations of naturalistic characters, they are employed, but not in any way that would subordinate characterization to plot or that would cheaply exploit the audience. The primacy of people determines his very play construction:

Subject matter stems from people. If people are interesting, their characters colorful with lights and shadows playing in their emotional corners, then exploring them becomes an adventure in drama. Having discovered my cast, I visualize them in surroundings, sometimes strange and piquant, at other times familiar and even nondescript.[15]

The irony of the "serious" critics' designation of faults in his construction is their unwillingness to accept Rattigan's plays on Rattigan's terms. Instead, they would fault him for using conventional techniques, but when those techniques were missing they would also react negatively. This pattern of criticism can be seen in the reviews of *First Episode, Flare Path,*

Adventure Story, and *Cause Célèbre,* among others. So, at the time that
Rattigan was criticized for being slick, fashionable, well-made, he was
accused of not being such. In a defensive statement of his own sense of firm
dramatic structure, Rattigan wrote:

The school of thought that condemns firm dramatic shape derives, I suppose,
originally from Tchekov, an author who, in my impertinent view, is not usually
properly understood either by his worshippers or his active imitators. I believe
that his plays are as firmly shaped as Ibsen's. The stream that seems to meander
its casual length along does so between strong artificial banks, most carefully
and cunningly contrived by a master craftsman. To admire the stream and ignore
the artifice that gave it its course seems to me a grave oversight, and may well
have led over the years to the present critical misapprehension by which laziness
of construction is thought a virtue and the shapelessness of a play is taken as
evidence of artistic integrity.[16]

Rattigan has drawn his characters from the stream of his own personal
life and dealt with them within the "banks" of conventional English
attitudes. When personal needs and desires of those characters are not
accommodated by existing social conventions, problems of pain, loneliness, and confusion result, and the streams overrun their banks. "He
chooses lost and confused people who are afraid of life. And in the last act
he reclaims them triumphantly through the sympathy of their neighbors.
He makes them feel they belong to the human race."[17] Polished without
being slick, natural without untidiness, Rattigan's art has given firm
shape to the mid-twentieth-century mainstream of English life, chronicling the sweeping changes in the moods and attitudes of the times, as did
Chekhov for his time. Rattigan's techniques followed recognizable dramatic lines without enslavement by them. Between the rigidities of the
well-made formula play and the freedoms of the experimental waves of
new dramas, his sense of theater remained firm, especially evident in the
increasing frankness with which he dramatized the most painful and the
most intimate experiences which since then have become accepted subjects
on the modern stage.

Chapter Three
Changing Times
New Theater Waves

In the middle decade of the twentieth century, three theatrical events occurred that marked the close of what had been called, rightfully or not, a twilight era of English drama and the beginning of an intoxicatingly experimental drama. First, on 22 September 1954, Terence Rattigan's major play, *Separate Tables,* opened at the St. James Theatre in London's West End, where it enjoyed a two-year run as Shaftesbury Avenue's major production. Two years later, on 5 May 1956, at the experimental, private-stage-company Royal Court Theatre, John Osborne's *Look Back in Anger,* with its disillusioned and very angry Jimmy Porter as hero, took the stage by storm and appeared to send the lonely, frustrated, but genteel characters of Rattigan's double bill to temporary seclusion in their Bournemouth hotel. Finally in 1957 and 1958 in production at small theaters in Bristol and Cambridge, Harold Pinter's *The Room* and *The Birthday Party* opened. All four plays are about isolated and trapped characters and the ways in which they deal with their pain in equally hostile environments. The settings are a shabbily genteel hotel, small and squalid apartments, and a dreary seaside hotel. Yet the unleashed fury of Osborne's intelligent, educated, lower-middle-class Porter and the bafflingly enigmatic theatrical style and characters of Pinter introduced to the English stage a drama that suddenly made Rattigan's Major Pollock and Miss Railton-Bell seem old-fashioned. Indeed, Rattigan's response to the disillusioned Jimmy Porter, for whom there were no more great causes, was that actors would measure their roles with the attitude of "Look, how unlike Terence Rattigan I'm being."[1] The gap between Rattigan, on the one hand, and Pinter-Osborne, on the other, seemed wide, and so overnight Rattigan found himself easily dismissed as old-fashioned, conventional, popular, well-made, entertaining, etc. It seemed that the twilight era of drama was at an end and that the new, "serious" drama would relegate the "theatre of

19

entertainment" to critical oblivion for at least twenty years. But critics and academicians notwithstanding, West End audiences continued to patronize Shaftesbury Avenue, while smaller audiences found their way to the subsidized or private theaters where the new plays were being staged. Division sharpened as the latter received most of the critical applause and the former, although prospering commercially, assumed in many instances an unjustified inferiority. The "absurd" and the "angry" theaters were new labels for plays of alienation and of social, political, and philosophical commitment during the twenty years that the full force of European dramatic influences—Beckett, Ionesco, Brecht—was felt in England.

Forerunners of the New

Yet, both the first and second waves of the new drama did not break without warning. Although the problem play and the drawing-room comedy, fashioned variously by Pinero, Wilde, Maugham, Galsworthy, and others, dominated London stages, attempts had been made, Rattigan wrote, to rescue the theater from the "thraldom of middle class vernacular in which it has been held . . . since Tom Robertson. . . ."[2] T. S. Eliot and Christopher Fry wrote poetic drama in their attempt to break the servitude to naturalistic subject matter and language. Peter Ustinov records an attempt to

form an English Playwrights' Company in emulation of the celebrated American producing organization run by the playwrights themselves: Elmer Rice, Maxwell Anderson, Sidney Howard, Robert E. Sherwood, and Marc Connelly. The British team was to be Priestley, Terence Rattigan, James Bridie, Benn Levy, and myself, and we had two meetings in Priestley's flat, under the chairmanship of Benn Levy, the bearded socialist parliamentarian and the dramatist husband of Constance Cummings.

We arrived at a purely financial consideration in the course of the agenda. Benn Levy said, "I think this is a matter which only applies to highly successful dramatics, but since we all live and write in hopes, I suppose we should have a ruling." At this point he addressed himself to Rattigan. "Terry, perhaps you would tell us in confidence your solution to this problem?"

Terence Rattigan never had time to answer, for Jack Priestley interrupted, his hackles halfway risen. "I think I ought to remind you, gentlemen, that I, too, have had my share of success. . . ."[3]

Success or failure, talk about a new theater did not produce it, and the new drama was destined for a long delay. Shaw and O'Casey were still the major dramatists, and their legacy of Ibsen-like dramas, reshaped to

British concerns, was still influencing the theater. Attempts at a revolution in the drama during this twilight era produced for the most part either the poetic drama of Eliot and Fry or the drawing-room comedies and problem plays of Maugham and Pinero. Noel Coward wrote bittersweet comedies about a limited upper-middle class, similar in subject to the marital problem plays of his predecessors. Yet a small revolution was happening in his quiet deemphasis of plot and his cameolike creation of characters and mood. The passing of the old and foreshadowing of the new are inherent in the very title of one of his last plays, *A Song at Twilight,* in which traditional well-made-play techniques are fused with a tastefully frank treatment of homosexual subject matter. John Russell Taylor described this play along "with Rattigan's *Man and Boy* as the first completely convincing, completely serious well-made play in the British theatre for more than half a century: since Galsworthy's *Loyalties.*"[4] Throughout his long career, Coward maintained an elegance of style in which he reshaped certain traditional techniques to suit his characters and their behavior codes. He is more clearly than Rattigan the last of a long tradition of modern dramatists established by Tom Robertson, Arthur Wing Pinero, Henry Arthur Jones, Granville Barker, John Galsworthy, Oscar Wilde, and Somerset Maugham. Coward's plays challenged traditional subject matter, at the same time adapting certain well-made techniques to do so.

Rattigan's Role in the Changing Scene

It is Rattigan, however, whose self-styled "sense of theatre" produced the most visible signs of innovation with his insistence on the primacy of character and narrative over ideas and with his interest in a broader spectrum of English society. University students, schoolboys and schoolmasters, writers and actors, laundresses and barmaids, men and boys, princes and showgirls, foreigners and Englishmen, the younger and older generations, the lower, middle, and upper classes: these are only some of the wide range of subjects from which he chose his characters. He wove them into entertaining narratives which do not conform to the mechanically plotted melodramas of Scribe; nor, as concerned as they may be with prevailing social problems, are they as interested in problems and ideas as Ibsen's and Shaw's plays seem to be, sometimes to the obscuring of the realistically human experiences of people.

Rather, Rattigan is in the old literary tradition of storytelling which relies on the life he observed around him from his early days at Harrow and on the events of the time, such as World War II, famous English court

SAINT PETER'S COLLEGE LIBRARY
JERSEY CITY, NEW JERSEY 07306

trials, as well as on historical figures from both the recent and distant past. Unlike Scribe's, his stories are not ends in themselves, and unlike Ibsen's and Shaw's, his plays are not vehicles for social criticism and ideas. Rather, the story serves as a natural device for the expression of his deeply compassionate concern for people and of the most delicate emotions of people beset with problems. For, "I still believe that the best plays are about people, not things. No one seems to have been able to disprove the simple fact that the best plays do have a strong story line and lively characters."[5]

Rattigan wrote plays that from his earliest days were phenomenally successful as, one after another, they broke existing attendance records. Scattered among four or five other modest productions, *French Without Tears, Flare Path, While the Sun Shines, Love in Idleness, The Winslow Boy,* and *The Browning Version* began his reputation as a one-man theatrical establishment, and he was proclaimed by the tabloids in the 1950s as "The Golden Boy." These plays were followed by a venture into history, *Adventure Story;* a Pinero-like problem play without a Pinero-like ending, *The Deep Blue Sea;* a fantasy-comedy "occasional" piece for the coronation of Queen Elizabeth II, *The Sleeping Prince.* Then, having already won the Ellen Terry award twice for *The Winslow Boy* and *The Browning Version,* Rattigan reached the peak of his dramatic career with *Separate Tables.* In both London and New York it received wide critical and popular acclaim.

Aunt Edna

But in a coincidence of events, John Osborne's *Look Back in Anger* opened at the end of the long two-year London run of *Separate Tables,* and in a dramatic coup d'etat, one era seemed ended and another begun. Suddenly Rattigan was labeled old-fashioned, well-made, audience-pleasing, as though to be all of these automatically made one an inferior playwright. Taunted and hurt by the labels, Rattigan used his fictional character, Aunt Edna, to represent the immortal and indispensable audience for whom he wrote and whose history goes back to the beginnings of Western drama in Greece. She was responsible for his financial success as she was responsible for the financial failure of others. In one of his prefaces, Rattigan wrote that she may attend Shakespearean or Beckettian plays, or, on the other hand, she may exercise faulty judgment from time to time, in either case not intellectualizing why she liked or disliked a performance. For she makes "only two basic demands of the theatre—first, that it excite her to laugh or to cry or to wonder what is going to happen next; and, second, that she can suspend her disbelief willingly and without effort. It's only

Aunt Edna's *emotions* that a playwright can hope to excite, because we know for sure that she does bring those to the theatre."[6] "She is bored by propaganda, enraged at being 'alienated,' loathes placards coming down and telling her what is going to happen next, hates a lot of philosophical talk on the stage with nothing happening at all, enjoys poetry only when it is dramatic and fine prose only when there is action to go with it. Her greatest joy is still and always will be for a good strong meaty plot told by good strong meaty characters."[7] Obviously Rattigan is referring to Shaw's theater of ideas, Brecht's propagandistic "placards coming down" (his use of legends) and, finally, Beckett's plotless, static drama with a "lot of philosophical talk" and "nothing happening." However, he qualifies his criticism by commenting earlier that Aunt Edna sometimes enjoys Pinter, Ionesco, Beckett, but when she does, it is because her emotions are stirred, "whether to tears or to laughter or to pure theatrical excitement. The three gentlemen named may well be highbrows themselves. That I would hardly know. I do know that their plays are not."[8]

In justification of his creation of Aunt Edna, Rattigan continues: ". . . Aunt Edna is a part of a majority audience for which true theatre exists, and has always existed; while highbrow theatre, if there were such a thing, would exist only for a minority audience, which is a euphemism for a small audience, which is a euphemism for . . . a play that should have been read and not acted, which is a euphemism for a flop."[9] In Rattigan's cleverly dramatized fictional trial of himself, the presiding judge reads some of the accusations leveled at the playwright: " 'He has an incurably second-rate mind.' Another: 'His plays are empty of all intellectual content whatever.' And yet another: 'The trouble with Mr. Rattigan is that he just cannot think.' Yes, Sir Robert, [the name of the case-winning lawyer of *The Winslow Boy*] that might explain your difficulty."[10] In another part of the trial Rattigan objects to the plaintiff's counsel's definition of the "thirties' drama as 'totally effete and degenerate,' " and to the view that "entertainment *per se* is necessarily an unworthy objective of drama."[11]

Using the trial to anthologize so many of his previous statements about the theater, Rattigan refers to the "compliment paid me of being pummelled on successive weeks by Benn Levy, James Bridie, Peter Ustinov, Sean O'Casey, Ted Willis, Christopher Fry and finally Bernard Shaw. Despite that I have always stuck firmly to that belief."[12] The pummeling is a reference to responses of these writers to Rattigan's attack on Shaw's theater of ideas in the *New Statesman*.

Throughout the twenty-year reign of the first and second waves of new English playwrights, Rattigan remained firm in his insistence on theater as entertainment (the moving to tears and laughter) by means of a good story. What he did not talk about until his last few years, however, are the complex problems that lie deeply rooted in the characters of his plays and the way in which his characters deal with the pain of those problems. Only after the censorship laws were revoked in 1968 was there official freedom, for example, to deal with homosexual problems. Yet Rattigan, having disguised these in some plays, openly dealt with the subject in *Man and Boy* as early as 1963. Even so, it is not the problems themselves that loom importantly in his dramas but the tears, laughter, and pain with which people faced and endured those problems. Audiences admired the characters and sympathized with their essentially courageous handling of the problems.

In fact, Rattigan's early concern with youthful sexual experiences (*First Episode*, 1934) and his vastly different means of handling these same experiences in his last play (*Cause Célèbre*, 1977) chronicle in dramatic form the changing times and attitudes of the World War II era, as well as those of the pre– and post– World War II periods. He managed, in addition, to triumph when in the 1970s—after the twenty-year waves of innovations had subsided into acceptance and, literally, into established theaters—his plays moved a new generation of jeans-clad audiences and younger critics.

In his *New Statesman and Nation* debate of 1950, in the prefaces to the first three volumes of his *Collected Plays*, and in the many interviews that he freely gave, Rattigan, above all else, respected audience desires without violating his own sense of theater. The huge audiences of Rattigan's distinguished career in the pre-1956 era, the successes he enjoyed as a screen writer, the many honors awarded him—two Ellen Terry Awards, the New York Drama Critics' Circle Award, the C.B.E., and in 1971 his knighting by Queen Elizabeth—his long associations with the most talented and glamorous people of his day, and finally his triumphant, if brief, return to the British stage: all these chronicle a fully realized career as "famous playwright," an ambition he dreamed about in his Harrow days.

Assimilation

Now that the new drama is no longer new and the seemingly infinite innovations of dramatic techniques have become customary and expected, even to Aunt Edna, synthesis in the theater has replaced divisiveness. Sociological, psychological, and philosophical dramatists with such labels as absurdists, social realists, kitchen-sink writers, dark fantastics who came from all directions—private stage companies, provincial theaters, theater workshops, radio and television—have been absorbed into English stage history. The distinction between the "popular" West End/ Shaftesbury, commercial offerings and those of the subsidized "serious" establishments has lost its edge. John Osborne and Harold Pinter, along with John Arden, Edward Bond, Shelagh Delaney, Simon Gray, Ann Jellicoe, David Hare, Henry Livings, David Mercer, John Mortimer, Peter Nichols, Joe Orton, David Rudkin, James Saunders, Anthony Shaffer, Peter Shaffer, N. F. Simpson, Tom Stoppard, David Storey, Arnold Wesker, John Whiting, Heathcote Williams, and many other new writers no longer seem revolutionary or sensational. Although not identified with the experiments in drama, Rattigan certainly will be remembered, as the London *Times* obituary headline reads, as "enduring" for many reasons, but perhaps most of all for his unique adaptation of certain well-made play techniques by means of which contemporary life was shaped for and, therefore, welcomed by large audiences. He is, perhaps, not so much the last of the well-made playwrights, as he and Noel Coward have often been labeled, but the first of the new, even as he adapted time-honored and recognizable dramatic techniques. But "old" and "new" are identifications which time itself makes meaningless.

About three months after Rattigan's death on 30 November 1977, Richard Gilman in a lead article of the *New York Times* arts section echoed the sentiment of many critics and historians in the title of his piece: "Out Goes Absurdism—In Comes the New Naturalism."[13] Whatever "new naturalism" may mean, it probably would include a variety of dramatic traditions more amenable to the Aunt Edna in all of us, the dramatic excitement of a well-told story and a well-made play.

The Scribean Well-Made Play

A brief note about the much used and abused term "the well-made play" is in order. It has been handy as a term of condescension or outright condemnation to describe a mechanically constructed formula play in the manner of its French masters, Scribe and Sardou. Certain ingredients, arranged in a highly patterned chronology of exposition, complication, climax, denouement, and conclusion, guaranteed a sure hit with audiences. The ingredients include

(1) a plot based on a secret known to the audience but withheld from certain characters (who have long been engaged in a battle of wits) until its revelation (or the direct consequence thereof) in the climactic scene serves to unmask a

fraudulent character and restore to good fortune the suffering hero, with whom
the audience has been made to sympathize; (2) a pattern of increasingly intense
action and suspense, prepared by exposition (this pattern assisted by contrived
entrances and exits, letters, and other devices); (3) a series of ups and downs in
the hero's fortunes, caused by his conflict with an adversary; (4) the counter-
punch of *peripeteia* and *scène à faire,* marking, respectively, the lowest and the
highest point in the hero's adventures, and brought about by the disclosure of
secrets to the opposing sides; (5) a central misunderstanding or *quidproquo,* made
obvious to the spectator but withheld from the participants; (6) a logical and
credible denouement; and (7) the reproduction of the overall action pattern in
the individual acts.[14]

The first act is usually slow, as the audience is given teasing bits of
information about the characters and situations, which are complicated (as
opposed to complex) by perfectly timed exits and entrances, frequently
through the requisite French window. "Toward the end the plot gathers
momentum with an important step taken by the hero. The succeeding acts
diminish in length and intensity. The final act discloses the withheld
secrets in a flurry of excitement."[15]

Ibsen, the oft-proclaimed father of the modern play, although breaking
away from the Scribean subject matter and techniques, utilized many
Scribean conventions for his socially significant drama. Shaw and O'Casey
broke even more with the formulaic French play, imaginatively adapting
some of its techniques. Even in the new wave of English drama in the late
1950s and 1960s critics increasingly have called attention to these techniques in the plays of Osborne, Pinter, and Orton. What some critics
referred to condescendingly, sometimes belittlingly, in the Scribean play
were the totally predictable plot and the mechanical manipulation of
characters. It became unfashionable, in some critical circles, to have any
plot at all. Equally unfashionable were characters with whom the audience
could sympathize. A time of protest, alienation, and paradox had set in.

In the theater of Sardou and Scribe

characters are puppets manipulated for the sake of creating a breathtaking
situation. Characters have a way of developing of their own accord and making
hay of a carefully prepared plot. This was the difficulty that Rattigan triumphed
over. He could bring living beings to the highest point of dramatic tension
without in any way violating the integrity of their personalities. Hester Collyer,
hopelessly in love in "The Deep Blue Sea" (1952), Andrew Crocker-Harris in
"The Browning Version" (1948), the harshness of his nature suddenly broken
down by a single set of kindness, the faded and bullied spinster who in "Separate

Tables" (1954) finds a companion in a most unlikely place; none of these ever forfeits the integrity of their reality for the sake of dramatic crisis; and dramatic crisis is never diminished by the integrity of their reality. This is Rattigan's unique achievement.[16]

The crisis or *scène à faire* of the French formula play is the supreme moment of tension in the play toward which plot and characters move and to which plot credibility and character honesty are frequently sacrificed. In Rattigan's plays, on the whole, dramatic crisis exists within the truth of the character, not as a manipulative effort to produce an artificial tension.

The Well-Made Problem Play

A second and much looser understanding of the well-made play would include the social problem dramas of writers like Pinero and Galsworthy, who used Scribean techniques to evoke pity for the victims of domestic problems and social injustices of various sorts. Although Rattigan dealt with similar problems, his characters for the most part do exercise free will. Consequently, even the most painfully unhappy characters, such as Hester Collyer, elicit as much admiration as pity in their courageous coping with problems and the consequences of their choices. For "Rattigan's outlook is essentially tragic," and "after the early plays, it is only in his films . . . that the gaiety of the jokes drown the deep moan of human unhappiness."[17] The distinction implied in this assertion by Hobson is the difference between pity, on the one hand, and pity mixed with admiration on the other. The first lacks tragic stature; the second strongly asserts this stature. The first negates life; the second affirms it. Rattigan's characters belong to the second group. Galsworthy's and Pinero's, with their strong sense of victimization, do not.

Rattigan's Well-Made Play

There is, still, a third definition, Rattigan's own, of the well-made play as opposed to the ill-made play. He constantly rejected the idea that craftsmanship is undesirable even though it may seem to be unfashionable. Whatever style the writer employs, total commitment and self-discipline are necessary. To young playwrights his advice is *"learn* your job."[18] "Terry is attuned to work only after long preliminaries and skirmishes. . . . He retouches and buffs his play as he goes along, sometimes crossing out a line dozens of times before he feels he has the right one. But this decision then becomes final; he does not alter it afterwards."[19] For to Rattigan "artistic construction is of the greatest interest . . . and even the *New Statesman* admits he knows all about the well-knit play. He studies Ibsen, Shaw, and Pinero for the way in which they create their effects, but he had learned from Shakespeare."[20]

Although Rattigan learned from the best playwrights, he did not imitate them and, consequently, found himself defending his plays against what he felt was misunderstanding. "Lately another malaise has upset the theatre: the vogue—in England as well as in America—for the 'ill-made play.' The 'well-made play' has become a term of abuse; we are still reacting against Arthur Wing Pinero and John Galsworthy, and the beams, nails and mortising that were so obvious in their dramaturgy. Tennessee Williams and Arthur Miller make their plays well, but they have concealed the architecture skillfully. Much critical writing to the contrary, Chekhov's are the best-made plays."[21] It is an ongoing tradition of drama with which Rattigan identifies his work, that largest of all traditions, which insists on the best workmanship and eventually the best utilization of talent one is capable of. From his influences—Shakespeare, Ibsen, Galsworthy, Shaw, Chekhov—he learned well. Combining these influences with his honesty, his painfully accurate observation of people in their times, his impeccably English manner and background, and most important of all, his overriding sense of theater, he met the real test of his heart in that "absolute stillness in the theatre when the truth is being told, when the audience recognize it and know. . . ."[22]

Like all enduring plays from the Greeks to the present, Rattigan's are well-made dramas as opposed to those that are ill-made. His narrative gift is directed toward finely grained studies of twentieth-century characters in the problematic context of their personal relationships. Craftsmanship and polish give his unique shape to the same people and the same world treated by John Osborne, Harold Pinter, and, one critic has mentioned, even Joe Orton. Chronicling the moods and problems of more than four decades of the mid-twentieth century, he has written twenty-four stage plays and has been involved in more than thirty film, television, and radio plays. His growth is measured by the increasingly complex characters and the constantly new subjects for his dramas, as events and changed social attitudes provided him with those subjects. Amidst changes, however, certain thematic concerns remain constant from his earliest plays: filial relations, social hypocrisies (especially in sexual matters), damaging emotional repressions, justice and a sense of what is right, a basic innocence reflected in his "schoolboy" characters as late as his last play, a sophistication and cynicism reflected in the tycoons and V.I.P.s of his film years, a lifelong fascination with history, a sympathetic tolerance for the foibles of foreigners and Englishmen. But perhaps most of all he cherished an elegance and good taste that are as at home with the cockney airman and the American showgirl as they are with writers, artists, cricketers, diplomats, and princes—the spectrum of the contemporary social structure that he knew so well. Just as his characters, from Margot in *First Episode* to Alma Rattenbury in *Cause Célèbre,* maintained dignity and composure in their humiliation, so Rattigan's well-made play (as opposed to the ill-made play) maintained its integrity through the turbulences of the mid-century English stage revolution.

The events of 1956 and 1957–58 seem to have changed English drama; more certainly they have made it more accessible to new techniques and subject matter. Yet, even Rattigan's earliest plays reflect some of the new subject matter, and they do illustrate a master's reshaping of a traditional style which held firmly through the changes. The 1970s have seen increasing revivals of well-made plays. Rattigan's last plays, *In Praise of Love* and *Cause Célèbre,* were a strong demonstration of a dramatic power that commanded audiences that had been weaned on Osborne and Pinter.

His contentious debate about Shaw's theater of ideas notwithstanding, Rattigan belongs in part to the tradition of Galsworthy and Shaw. Linked frequently with Coward as the last of the well-made playwrights, he claims Chekhov as his teacher in scene construction and in his emphasis on the implicit rather than the explicit. Like Osborne and Pinter, Rattigan is concerned with deeply personal problems of love, sex, and marriage. In the resolutions of his problems he is Chekhovian in the way in which his characters endure in their lives, without melodramatic endings and without total victimization by society. Ultimately the character bears responsibility for his life and deals honestly with his own truth with the maximum dignity he can muster. Realistic in his outlook, Rattigan does not opt for happy endings. On the other hand, as an affirmer of life, he shuns the alienation from society and life that characterizes so many modern dramatic characters. His affirmations are those of the kind that only the tragic sense can provide.

Now that the alienated characters of the revolutionary drama have lost their newness and provocativeness and have been absorbed into the dramatic mainstream, divisive labels, such as "drawing room" and "kitchen sink" plays, have shed their judgmental inferences. They are merely terms designating dramatic trends in the mid-twentieth century. In fact, as far back as 1961, recognition of the new and the old is seen in one of the more balanced views of the London theater season:

> Still another "new wave"—playwrights like Arnold Wesker and Harold Pinter, actors like Peter Woodthorpe and Peter O'Toole—have added their names to an illustrious youth movement headed by Osborne, Behan, Delaney and Plowright; and the year also brought new triumphs for veterans like Rattigan and Guinness.[23]

At the conclusion of *The Rise and Fall of the Well Made Play* John Russell Taylor reports an incident that bespeaks the legacy Rattigan left to the English stage. In the audience-reaction portion of a theater symposium, one lady (she may very well be Aunt Edna) said she "just wanted a good laugh, a good cry and either way a good story in the theatre: she berated us for not caring about the needs of such people, and clearly did not believe our protestations that we [symposium participants] did, very much. But when the audience had gone and the speakers were relaxing over a cup of tea conversation turned to what had first got us excited by the theatre: *A Streetcar Named Desire,* volunteered one, *Ring Round the Moon* ventured another. There was an appreciative pause. Another piped up, '*The Deep Blue Sea*—now *there* was a play for you. . . .' "[24] Rattigan's sense of the theater, which never forgot the presence of an audience, is the main reason that even his most serious dramas entertained the audiences, and in the long run it is the ability to do so that determines enduring theater.

Chapter Four
First Episodes

Summing up his early reputation as a popular dramatist, Rattigan, in 1953, the year of his occasional play written for Queen Elizabeth's coronation (*The Sleeping Prince*), amiably catalogued his successes:

Two of them, *French Without Tears* and *While the Sun Shines*, both played for over a thousand performances, and I have it on the authority of the late Mr. John Parker, the omniscient editor of *Who's Who in the Theatre*, that, on those grounds, I can lay claim to a sort of world's record, in that I am apparently the only playwright, until now, who has written two plays so blessed with longevity. *Flare Path* ran for eighteen months, *The Winslow Boy* for fifteen, and *Love in Idleness*, after a season in London limited first to three months and then extended to six, survived nearly two years on Broadway.[1]

Comprising Volume 1 of his *Collected Plays*, published in 1953, the above-mentioned are only five of ten plays he had written by 1946. Among the early uncollected plays, he chose to publish only one, *After the Dance*, in a single edition and in an anthology. The other four remain unpublished. All four were written in collaboration with various friends: *First Episode* with Philip Heimann, an adaptation of *A Tale of Two Cities* with John Gielgud, *Follow My Leader* with Anthony Maurice (Tony Goldschmidt), and *Grey Farm* with Hector Bolitho. For whatever reasons Rattigan did not include some early plays in the collected edition, they are important as modest beginnings and for their thematic and stylistic qualities developed in subsequent dramas.

Two which merit particular attention are *First Episode* and *After the Dance*, the first because of its discovery in 1977 by Michael Darlow and Gillian Hodson and, subsequently, the purchase of its production option by Naim Attallah and, also, because of the renewed interest in Rattigan's plays in the 1970s, especially regarding the disguised homosexuality in his early dramas. The second of the two plays, however, is a complete and satisfying serious drama, deserving of more than the brief run it enjoyed in

31

1939 when the dark events of World War II figured in its shortlived stage run.

Events of the time determined in curiously ironic ways the fate of a number of Rattigan's plays, among which was another early work, *Follow My Leader,* a farcical satire about Hitler, banned in 1938 and than allowed production in 1940. To the period of the early 1930s also belongs an unpublished drama, *A Tale of Two Cities,* whose conflict with another dramatization of the Dickens novel resulted in the cancellation of its production and indirectly in the later acceptance of Rattigan's oft-rejected manuscript of *French Without Tears,* whose potential disaster and actual success are now stage history.

First Episode

First Episode, Rattigan's first professionally produced play, opened in London in 1934 and in New York later that same year. To the American reviewer Brooks Atkinson, the play "has something to say that might be worth listening to," but the authors "barely state it" and "do not develop it in their characterization, which would be the normal way to treat it." Instead, they stir it up "with some pretty intolerable scenes of undergraduate horseplay and dissipation."[2] To a London reviewer, the "impression is that at least half a dozen minds must be at work, each pulling a different way, so oddly irregular is the play's movement and so constantly shifting is its centre of interest. . . . And for all its somewhat self-conscious vulgarities, the farce is alive. . . . The shock-headed 'muff' of Mr. Angus, though it is a minor part, is more alive than any other character."[3]

Of particular interest in the reviews are the references to the shifting of focus and the strength of minor roles, for these are characteristics of Rattigan's style which he continued in much of his writing and which critics continued to draw attention to as weaknesses.

Drawn from Oxford undergraduate life, *First Episode* is a "rites of passage" play involving a close friendship between David Lister and Tony Wodehouse and an interruption of that friendship by Margot Gresham, an older actress, who comes to Oxford to play Cleopatra. Tony's current liaison with Joan, a mindless younger actress, has been losing its attraction for him, and Margot provides him with a diversion. However, the diversion takes a more serious turn as Tony thinks that he is in love with Margot's mind as well as her body. Gradually he discovers his delusion as he becomes irritated by her possessiveness and as David, self-appointed protector of Tony, helps end the relationship. Margot at the end realizes that, although for her the romance is a serious one, for Tony it is just an episode.

The triangular situation becomes acute when Margot, out of anger at David, informs a proctor of David's presence in Joan's room, a violation of university rules which causes David's expulsion from Oxford. In the end David accepts his punishment gracefully, and Tony generously understands Margot's motive. In her apology to David she repeats his earlier assertion that the friendship between the two men is impregnable. The breaking up of the liaison reinforces another statement of David's, that heterosexual liaisons are primarily physical ones. Undergraduate jokes about sex rearing its ugly head in the male paradise turn serious as Tony finds himself having to lie to Margot and to tolerate her jealousy of David. The undergraduate Eden is described at one point as "this cozy little nook, and our happy little circle, you at your books and Bertie addressing his envelopes, and Philip deep in his 'Sporting Life' by the fireside."[4]

If Margot is jealous of David's hold on Tony, David equally resents her possessiveness of Tony and admits that his dislike of her is due to her threat to the male friendships. In a crossed-out passage in the play manuscript, David asks Tony whether Margot knows "about us." The lines may be read as physical or platonic preference and are an example of Rattigan's oblique handling of sexual subject matter.

The autobiographical sources for the play are strong. During his Oxford days, Rattigan lived in the Canters house with Philip Heimann and others, just as in the play David, Tony, Philip, and Bertie share a house. At Oxford Rattigan had a one-line part in *Romeo and Juliet,* directed by John Gielgud and starring Edith Evans and Peggy Ashcroft (whose name evokes Margot Gresham's). It was Gielgud's first directorial experience in a Shakespearean play, and in *First Episode* Margot plays her first Shakespearean role. Rattigan's transmuting of his experiences into art is apparent in such specific instances.

Moreover, David Lister plans to become a famous journalist, as Rattigan dreamed of becoming a "famous playwrite." Both David and Tony rebel against their fathers' ambitions for their careers, as Rattigan and Heimann opposed paternal plans. In a more intimate way, Margot's threat to David's friendship with Tony bears resemblance to Heimann's serious liaison with an older woman whom he later married.

But the autobiographical parallels are subsumed in the larger issues of the play, issues which consistently reappear in Rattigan's later dramas. Close male friendships, unequal romances between an older and a younger person with one feeling deeply the need to give and the other to receive love, filial conflicts, the growth of boy into man, the frustrations and pains as innocence gives way to experience leaving in its wake deep ambivalences—these profoundly human situations increase and intensify with almost every play Rattigan wrote.

It was the farcical scenes of undergraduate life, however, which most reviewers approved as they minimized the serious themes and characters. Undergraduate horseplay with scenes of drinking, gambling, weekend romances, cricket, and in general the carefree idyll that undergraduate life involves provided the "liveliness to cover its rather more than occasional failure to make its development plausible."[5]

"They're entertaining, but . . ." became for some critics the standard response to many of Rattigan's dramas.

In regard to the "shift of focus" in *First Episode* referred to by critics, there is possibly the problem of looseness, as each of the three acts is built around a different character: David in Act I, Margot in Act II, and Tony in Act III. The actions of each, however, implicitly converge to the final scene of the play, in which David, Margot, and Tony share equal importance. Normally Margot and Tony would say their farewells in private. Here, however, in David's presence, she kisses Tony and then wordlessly leaves. Tony merely asks David if she has gone, and David replies, "Yes—she's gone." The curtain falls. There is no doubt that, in spite of his being "sent down," David is the victor. David's triumph over Margot is handled by Rattigan with minimal theatricality and with maximum implicitness. It is this tautness of style that gives Rattigan's language its extraordinarily modern tone. In the end, the play for all its apparent shift of focus is not loose. If each scene is developed around people, as Rattigan asserts, the threads of the relationships among those people are woven firmly at the play's end. The unity of the play resides in the implicit tightening of the narrative threads.

Rattigan's insistence on implicitness is further evidenced in the deliberate, educated flatness with which his middle-class characters speak. When Tony returns from rehearsal and talks about his love for Margot, David's response is a subtextual one, as the unspoken meaning leaps from his spoken words: "Her eyes are too close together. . . . Her mouth too small, and I don't like her voice." "Did you have a good rehearsal?"[6] One knows immediately that it is for deeper reasons than eyes and mouth that David dislikes Margot. The tension between outer details and inner feelings permeates Rattigan's characterizations with conflicts and ambivalences. Popular audiences identify with them instinctively; more critical audiences appreciate the implicitness; the actor manipulates this language for maximum effect.

For a 1933 production, *First Episode* was ahead of its time in the dramatization of a battle between a man and woman for the attention of another man, even though sexual subjects were under the scrutiny of the Lord Chamberlain. "When I started in the theatre, one was perhaps too anxious to succeed, and not to offend," Rattigan later said.[7] In its sexual battles, the play looks ahead to more open treatments of this particular kind of romantic triangle in plays like Pinter's *The Collection* and his film play of Robin Maugham's *The Servant*. The entanglements contain conflicts between heterosexual and homosexual attractions and between older and younger persons.

Three Minor Plays

Rattigan's next play, and his second collaboration, was the adaptation with John Gielgud of *A Tale of Two Cities*. He was paid fifty pounds for the script. Gielgud was to play the dual roles of Sidney Carton and the Marquis St. Evremonde, but the play was put aside because Bronson Albery, manager of the New Theatre, had a project underway involving Sir John Martin Harvey, a seventy-year-old actor who was "planning to play Sidney Carton himself in a farewell tour of his adaptation of the novel."[8] Out of consideration for the actor, Rattigan and Gielgud's adaptation was shelved. But Albery asked Rattigan to send him any other play he might write, and the consequence of the invitation was Albery's purchase of the six-times-rejected *French Without Tears*, Rattigan's first smash hit.

Although *French Without Tears* chronologically follows *First Episode*, discussion of it will be deferred so that the remainder of the uncollected or unpublished plays can be discussed.

Follow My Leader, written in collaboration with Anthony Maurice, is a Chaplinesque satire on Hitler, its production banned in 1938 for political censorship reasons which as late as 1957 roused Rattigan's blood. When allowed production in 1940, the farce was generally received as an entertainment that "succeeds in being good fun," but there was one stroke of brilliant farce that caught the reviewer's attention. "The British Ambassador, who has just been blown up in his Embassy, comes in clothes that, though torn and dusty, are still correct, to draw the foreign Minister's attention to the irregularity. Mr. Marcus Barron's studied vagueness is a

perfect piece of playing, and his departure with the promise of an impartial
investigation is made to seem a diplomatic triumph."[9]

Follow My Leader is the story of a simple-witted plumber who is made a
dummy dictator to resolve the rivalry of the Party's two real leaders. The
"sight of the poor lumpen-Hitler before the microphone, yelling the
ferocious harangues that a lounging secretary dictates to him sentence by
sentence makes an amusing picture that the authors exploit to the fullest
possible extent."[10] Finally, the *Times* reviewer concludes, "*Follow My
Leader* succeeds in being good fun; but one is surprised that the author of
French Without Tears could do no better than Ruritania without overmuch
laughter."[11]

Least of the minor early plays of Rattigan and seen only in New York,
Grey Farm is a grotesque story about a psychopathic murderer, James
Grantham (who strangles a servant girl behind the arras), and his relationship with his son. Its grim, humorless psychological study of a father-son
relationship contrasts strangely with the comic freshness of *First Episode,*
the farcical mood of *French Without Tears,* and the muted, gray, Chekhovian atmosphere of *After the Dance.* Written in collaboration with Hector
Bolitho, a popular novelist of the time, its failure may be explained at least
partly in a comment by David in *After the Dance.* Peter, David's secretary,
asks why the "stuff they had written the previous night wasn't to David's
liking, since he thought it read rather well." David replies, "That's just
the trouble with it. It reads too well—imitation Hector Bolitho."[12] David
asserts that he is not writing history to be read by the sort of people who
read Hector Bolitho.

After the Dance

Of these early uncollected plays, *After the Dance* is the only one that has
been published. It is a somber sequel to the earlier treatments of undergraduate life. Two generations are represented in the characters, one "now
of an age to be conscripted" and the other who "were drinking youthful
cocktails when the late War ended."[13] Together they establish a mood like
that in Chekhov's *Cherry Orchard,* set in a time suspended between past
and future, a stalemated present. It is also the mood of Shaw's *Heartbreak
House,* in which only the falling bomb at the end provides the occupants
with an exhilarating release from the oppressiveness of the present. The
major character is David, an historian, who dictates to Peter, his secretary:
"It was a time when Europe still lay under the dark shadow cast by the

giant figure of Prince Metternich; when the twin forces of nationalism and liberalism had not yet dared show their heads. . . ."[14] The historical period David writes about is similar in mood to his own pre–World War II era.

David's loosely run household includes his wife of twelve years, Joan; their mutual friend, John, who is the only person Joan can communicate with; David's secretary, Peter, a younger man. Intruding on this familial group is Helen, Peter's friend, who falls in love with David and goes about her self-assumed duty of curing David's alcoholism. She enlists the medical assistance of her brother George, who diagnoses the writer's condition as cirrhosis. Meanwhile, Joan and John watch helplessly as Helen breaks relationships between David and Joan and between David and Peter.

Joan loves David very much but is unable to demonstrate or articulate her love, except to John. So she attends parties and fills her time buying small toys at Woolworth's for her friends. After her second-act suicide, John leaves, hoping to find a job and taking with him the celluloid duck Joan had given him.

In David, the pervasive aimlessness and frustrations of a generation between the two world wars find expression in his drinking, his attraction to Helen, and finally, in his peevishness with Peter, who is accused by David of collaborating rather than just typing.

Helen, on the other hand, is energetic and idealistic as the older generation is not; yet her actions at times seem insensitive and crude. Like Natasha in *The Three Sisters* and Lopahin in *The Cherry Orchard* and like Elly Dunn in Shaw's Chekhovian *Heartbreak House,* Helen is the active force for change. Like Checkhov's, Rattigan's characters do not change. Rather, they reveal their states of being, a phrase used by critics to describe the Russian playwright's character realizations.

Although the plot summary may seem melodramatic, the drama moves far beyond the sentimental world of melodrama. For it is a drama of mood and character, served well by a story narrated in small scenes. The mood is a Chekhovian gray, as people talk, laugh, and drink to disguise their deep boredom and pain. Their states of being in all their shaded and mixed natures are revealed by means of the narrative. Plot is handmaiden to character, unlike the technique of the formulaic well-made play. And the emotional colors are not sharp and clear. "I can't accept that things can be black and white; there are always tones of grey,"[15] Rattigan has said.

Although the drama contains the indefiniteness of life in its substance, its structural lines are quite clear. Each act, for example, contains the pattern of the overall action of the play. At the end of Act I, Helen and David decide to announce their love for each other, yet unforeseen circumstances preclude that announcement. Act II concludes quietly with an announcement, instead, of Joan's suicidal offstage fall from a balcony. At the end of Act III David cancels his dinner engagement with Helen in favor of going alone to the kind of party he and Joan used to attend, the kind with which Joan used to fill her empty existence. Each of the act endings effectively conveys the grays rather than the blacks and whites of life. Yet, like Chekhov, Rattigan affirms life in the resumption and continuity of things.

The *New York Times* reviewer wrote of Rattigan's "rare quality of not playing all his cards at once. Mr. Rattigan's people grow and change before your eyes, and their development is so fully traced that what is revealed of them in the third act is, when it comes, completely satisfying as a fulfillment of the hints given about them at the outset. We have not only a successful writer of farce but a dramatist of serious consequences." The *Times* reviewer concluded that "Mr. Rattigan's estimates of character are never fiercely prejudiced, and his method of allowing his people gradually to reveal themselves gives to his play a genuine distinction."[16]

As in *First Episode,* the focus seems to shift from Joan to John and then to David, with the growing, if negative, emphasis on Helen. In fact, the *New Statesman* reviewer suggested that "if the third act had been the first, we could have been shown this romance being deflated, as a direct result of the differing values accepted by the two generations, and thus the theme could have been properly illuminated."[17] Actually, however, the so-called differing values are merely contrasting parts of the same mood, the need to disguise in order to continue living. Helen's opportunism masquerades as energetic reform, and Joan's frustrations are disguised in her generous and tolerant behavior. The moral solemnity of the young and the masks of flippancy and boredom of the older characters create a paradox out of which inner conflicts grow and to which there are no easy or immediate solutions.

The suggested restructuring of the acts ignores the technical terms which Rattigan has chosen. The revision might well suit a plot in Galsworthy or Pinero but would violate the naturalistic indeterminateness with which Rattigan ends his plays. As in Chekhov's plays, no one seems able to make satisfying emotional connections, but, except for Joan, they do carry on. Rattigan as an artist in control of his creations is a craftsman who shapes his observation of humanity truthfully. ". . . where he is quietly drawing his major characters, he reveals himself as a serious dramatist of genuine insight, who can write light dialogue that is never an interpolated comic relief, but is always contributory to our knowledge of the mentality of the speakers."[18] And it is by this quiet drawing of characters through the device of narrative that Rattigan is reshaping familiar narrative technique to his unique dramatic purpose.

Of Rattigan's early minor plays, *First Episode* and *After the Dance* deserve revivals. The former would be interesting in the context of the new thematic freedoms of the stage, and the latter, unhampered by the threatening events which in 1939 probably cut short its run, would fare well in another time. It re-creates sharply the mood of a stalemated present caught between the past and future, a universality dramatized in earlier plays by Chekhov and Shaw.

Chapter Five
Major Success:
French Without Tears

Reception

Standing out among five early plays by virtue of the phenomenal box-office success it enjoyed both in England and abroad, *French Without Tears* with one stroke established Rattigan's reputation as a writer of light comedies. Opening on 6 November 1936, at the Criterion Theatre, London, it ran for 1,039 performances, with Kay Hammond, Jessica Tandy, Roland Culver, and Rex Harrison. The play was then produced in Sweden, the Netherlands, Austria, Hungary, Germany, and New Zealand. There seemed no end to its popularity. ". . . But then after it became a success people thought I could write only light comedies."[1] Rattigan would wait ten years until *The Winslow Boy* (1946) in similar overnight manner earned for him instant recognition as a writer of serious drama.

Described by John Russell Taylor as "one of the most spectacular successes of his whole spectacularly successful career,"[2] *French Without Tears* was built, according to Rattigan, "totally on a Chekhov pattern—very short scenes, no single star roles, a lot of duologues. . . ."[3] Like the much-written-about plotless play of Chekhov, this drama has little plot. There are merely a series of scenes unified by a *femme fatale* who exercises her charms alternately on three of the students. There is no single leading character, except for the fact that one of the students, Alan, takes himself more seriously than the others with his announced intention of becoming a writer rather than a diplomat.

In addition to Chekhov, Rattigan included Shaw as an early dramatic influence, and in this play certain overtones of Shaw are clearly there, particularly in the crisp, adroitly handled dialogue. Much of the humor of the play grows out of the fumbling use of French by beginning students. Laughter occurs immediately in the opening lines of the play involving the literal use of *gare* (French for "railway station") to mean "station of life." The linguistic laughs continue throughout the play.

The play, about student life and romance in a foreign-language school on the French Riviera, is a comedy performed frequently in provincial theaters. A production in 1974 by the Young Vic Company in London was reviewed by Clive Barnes, who said that he, in spite of being in three minds about the piece, "laughed, and there was much in the evening I enjoyed, particularly the staging and the acting."[4] The usual reluctance of some critics not to credit the play, but rather the acting/staging, ignores the possibility that, after nearly fifty years, the holding power of the comedy for both the young generation of actors and the middle-aged critics may reflect merit in the play itself. One can only speculate on how the revival of much less produced early plays such as *First Episode* and *After the Dance* would affect new generations of players and critics.

Plot Summary

The characters in the play are a group of young prospective diplomats studying French at the Riviera home of the master. The French master's daughter, Jacqueline, assists him and also serves a romantic interest in the sketchy plot. Diana, a seductress, is there only because her family is in India and her brother Kenneth is one of the students. She manages to enjoy the attentions of Kit, with whom Jacqueline is in love and who eventually discovers that he is being used by Diana. Commander Rogers, like Kit only too easily ensnared by Diana's charm, also finds out the true nature of Diana's attentions to him. Finally there is Alan, the student whose writing interests eventually win over his parent's wishes that he go into the diplomatic service and who unsuccessfully attempts to resist Diana's charms.

At one crucial moment in the play, Diana enters through the French window as Kit, Alan, and Rogers have found out that she is playing a cat-and-mouse game with them. Confronted with a question about the object of her real affection, she promptly confesses her love for Alan. In the fashion of John Tanner of Shaw's *Man and Superman,* Alan protests very strongly, and when he eventually renounces diplomacy in favor of writing and announces his plans to return to England, she partially gives up on him. But in Act III, with the appearance of Lord Heybrook (the new student talked about in Act I, who turns out to be fifteen years old), Diana with her usual composure calls, "Come and help me pack, someone. I'm going to catch that London train or die." Alan, pursuing her despairingly, cries, "No, no, oh, God, no! (*Turning at door*) Stop laughing, you idiots. It isn't funny. It's a bloody tragedy."[5]

In discussing with Kit and Rogers his romantic principles and ideals, particularly in regard to the girl he should like to fall in love with, Alan declares that she first of all must not be a cow, and "Secondly, she will be able to converse freely and intelligently with me on all subjects—Politics—Philosophy—Religion—Thirdly, she will have all the masculine virtues and none of the feminine vices. Fourthly, she will be physically unattractive enough to keep her faithful to me, and attractive enough to make me desire her. Fifthly, she will be in love with me. That's all, I think."[6]

Later in the same scene when Diana reveals Alan as her choice among the students, she and Alan go through a John Tanner–Ann Whitefield–like scene from Shaw's *Man and Superman*:

Alan: (*In agony.*) Oh, go away, Please go away.
Diana: All right. I know you have every right to think I'm lying, but I'm not, Alan, really I'm not. That's what's so funny.
Alan: (*Imploringly.*) Oh, God help me!
Diana: (*At door.*) Good night, Alan. (*Simply.*) I do love you. *She smiles tearfully at him. He throws away his cigarette, and walks over to her.*
Alan: Say that again, blast you!
Diana: I love you.
He embraces her fervently.
Diana: (*Emerging from embrace, ecstatically.*) I suppose this is true.
Alan: You know damn well it is.
Diana: Say it, darling.
Alan: (*Hedging.*) Say what?
Diana: Say you love me.
Alan: Must I? Oh, this is hell! (*Shouting.*) I love you.[7]

Diana's life force eventually captures Alan. Referred to as a bitch at the height of Alan's resistance to her, she manages throughout to maintain her good breeding and composure. She knows whom she wants, as Shaw's Ann Whitefield does, and one assumes that she may realize her desires. Although the ending of the play is indeterminate, she decides to follow Alan to London upon finding that Lord Heybrook is so young. She is the recurrent *femme fatale* figure in Rattigan's plays that reaches full dramatization in Lady Hamilton (*A Bequest to the Nation*).

But it is the male characters on whom Rattigan focuses sharply. All the men, but particularly Alan, Kit, and Rogers, form a close attachment. In fact, what Alan includes in the description of his ideal female are the characteristics that make a male friendship. His ideal is really a composite male. The attraction to Diana which he attempts to resist does not consist, as he so adamantly insists it should, of free conversing about politics, philosophy, and religion. And she is too attractive to be his ideal love. Too late does he realize his problem contained in that last line of the play in which he describes his plight as a "bloody tragedy." Underneath the farcical moments of the romantic entanglements there is a thin veil of potential romantic disillusionment continued from *First Episode* and *After the Dance,* which appears later in more complex form in characters such as Hester Collyer of *The Deep Blue Sea.*

The scale of the play is not a large one. In the youthful, carefree existence of students from privileged backgrounds, the most momentous problems faced are those involving learning French. The extracurricular activities involving Diana, Jacqueline, or the ladies of the town are romps as yet untouched by complex marital problems or by events of World War II which will soon take over center stage in Rattigan's plays. There is, equally, no concern with social or political problems with which Pinero and Shaw had been so involved or with the frustrations of the post–World War II era of Osborne's Jimmy Porter. Theirs is an idyllic existence. Soon, as in *After the Dance,* this generation will feel the boredom and apathy of the prewar years, then in *Flare Path* the problems of the war years, and in plays such as *Separate Tables* the intimately personal complexities of mature experiences in the postwar period. Within the small dimensions of the play it is a satisfying and enjoyable comedy, so that even a sophisticated critic in 1974 finds himself moved to laughter.

Style

As the first solo play by Rattigan, it is remarkably well made, a style that suits well its subject matter, even though the well-made label that was applied negatively to so much of his writing became the source of irritation to him. From the opening scene exploding with the laughter created by the misuse of "au-dessus sa gare" to the Frenchmaster's welcome in French to Lord Heybrook at the end, the dialogue sparkles with wittily humorous lines, undergraduate though some of that humor may be. No matter what happens, the characters do not lose their composure, right down to that final appearance of young Lord Heybrook. Small as the scale of comedy may be, it does not pretend to be anything more than the entertainment it is.

For all the Chekhovian and Shavian touches in the drama, the uses of the Scribean well-timed exits and entrances through the French windows earned instantly for him a reputation as a "French-window" or "drawing-room" dramatist by critics. Also, the overall pattern of the total play is evident in each act, particularly in the act endings. At the end of Act I there is reference to Jacqueline's changing her hair style to resemble Diana's so that Kit may notice her. At the end of Act II, the men leave for the town carnival minus the company of Diana, after a series of light-hearted complications about who would be her escort. These incidents anticipate Alan's departure from the school and from Diana, and they lead as well to the timely arrival of Lord Heybrook, who in Act I is briefly referred to as another possible conquest for Diana.

Themes

In addition to the Chekhov-Shaw influences and adroit deployment of some well-made-play qualities, there are those themes that have become hallmarks of Rattigan's popular plays: English schoolboys, foreigners, foreign languages and customs, diplomats, servicemen, nobility/royalty, ill-matched lovers, the undergraduate horseplay. Most importantly, however, for all the undergraduate antics of the students, they retain those essentially English upper-middle-class qualities: impeccable manners and composure, particularly the ease with which characters extricate themselves from entanglements and, in general, practice the gentlemanly arts and civilized sensibilities. A familiar pattern of names that graced Rattigan's plays was begun in this production, with Roland Culver, who played so many Rattigan roles and Rex Harrison, who appeared in the American production of *In Praise of Love* nearly four decades later.

The play ran for over a thousand performances in its initial 1936 production. Clive Barnes described its 1974 revival by the Young Vic as a delicious rebaked eclair which Mr. Dunlop (director) "sensibly approaches from a distance and crawls toward it with a crablike ambiguity. He stresses the artificiality of the piece, so that over the entire play there tastefully lurks that unasked, and certainly unanswered, question: 'Anyone for tennis?' "[8] It is thoroughly English. It is that essential English world (reflected tragically in his "serious" plays) in which the "spectre of defeat and disillusionment was banished, ultimately, to the limbo whence it came to be replaced by sanity attired in humour, in a world recivilized . . . by 'laughter learned of friends, by laughter too, as taught by Terry, and by—this, above all—gentleness—that last word 'gentleness' being the key, perhaps, to all he was and all he wrote."[9] Even in the carefree, idyllic "romp" of English students in a French-language school on the Riviera this English world, a wistful Chekhovian world, exists.

Language

One remaining point about this first hugely successful play of Rattigan's is in order, and it is a point about which Rattigan has commented defensively. Shunning what he termed the naturalistic vernacular of Robertson and, on the other hand, the poetic language of Eliot and Fry, he designated his language style as "everyday speech." This everyday speech seems flat, understated, unsuggestive according to William Douglas Home, an "unflamboyant rocket-stick! But when the match is lit, the fuse ignited, what a pay-off there is—rocket chasing rocket round the heavens, streamer chasing streamer, while the sky (to quote another dramatist of note) is 'painted with unnumbered sparks—and every one doth shine.' "[10] Home illustrates Rattigan's language from a line in *French Without Tears* in which Alan (Rex Harrison) reacts to a naval tale told by Rogers (Roland Culver) in which he had to call all hands on deck. Alan responds to this tale with an unanswered question: "and did they come?" Wordlessly Rollie "merely raised an eyebrow, in disgust and disbelief that anyone, even so flippant a character as Rex, could bring himself to ask it."[11] There is the "astonishing potential for development contained in every phrase he wrote, the stimulus to the imagination which he brought to bear unerringly on any audience."[12] Rattigan firmly believed that "the weapons of understatement and suggestions are even more effective in comedy than in tragedy,"[13] and that he had "with diligence, discipline, and self-restraint always practised the belief. In so far as this theory of comedy ran counter to the accepted critical opinion . . . [he can] therefore justify the claim . . . [he had] made . . . that the three comedies in this book had in them a small element of pioneering and experiment."[14] "Has not sense of theatre then something to do with the ability to thrill an audience by the mere power of suggestion, to move it by words unspoken, rather than spoken, to gain tears by a simple adverb repeated five times or in terms of comedy to arouse laughter by a glance or a nod? Surely, in comedy as in tragedy, it is the implicit rather than the explicit that gives life to a scene and, by demanding the collaboration of an audience, holds it, contented, flattered, alert and responsive."[15] Rattigan's comments on the unspoken language of drama suggest the usage by Chekhov and certainly by Pinter, who relied so heavily on silences. With Rattigan, however, it is the intonation, timing, and gesture which suggest the meaning more than the pauses and silences as in Chekhov and Pinter.

For all of its light thematic matter and its deceptively traditional style, *French Without Tears* is significant as Rattigan's first highly successful play and as an indicator of the qualities deepened and reshaped in later dramas.

Chapter Six

A Trilogy for World War II

Flare Path: A War Drama

According to Rattigan, his "intense longing to be taken seriously as a professional playwright" remained "unfulfilled for six long years, until in the intervals of whirling about over the South Atlantic in uneventful search of seemingly non-existent submarines, I wrote *Flare Path,* and later found myself on leave in London to attend its first night at the Apollo Theatre."[1] Gratified that "at long last I found myself commended, if not exactly as a professional playwright, at least as a promising apprentice who had definitely begun to learn the rudiments of his job,"[2] Rattigan began a series of stageplays and films about life during World War II. *Flare Path* (1942) was his first.

The carefree undergraduates of *French Without Tears* in 1936 and the prewar generation of *After the Dance* in 1939 have now matured and are facing problems of life and death in the dangerous bombing missions flown from an English air base. Less than perfectly matched marriages and romantic liaisons are undergoing the additional strains that accompany war times. The "grand hotel" setting here is a rather shabby, small hotel where airmen's wives wait for their husbands to return from missions and serves well the author's purpose of gathering in one place a variety of character types. Like *French Without Tears* earlier and *Separate Tables* a decade later, the framework device in *Flare Path* makes possible a richness of characterizations present in the oldest and best storytellers, such as Chaucer, and in modern times Gorki (*The Lower Depths*), O'Neill (*The Iceman Cometh*) and Pinter (*The Birthday Party*).

The bombing missions and air-force life in general create the dramatic tensions and excitement of the play. These are entangled with the marital situations of three couples, each a complete story in itself. The serious interest, however, is the triangular romance of Patricia, an English actress, her airman husband, Teddy, and Peter Kyle, an English-turned-American actor, now forty seven, with whom Patricia had once enjoyed an affair during her appearance with him in a New York play. Almost immediately Peter seems out of place in this wartime society in which people from disparate backgrounds are bound by a common cause that excludes those not involved in the war. Patricia still harbors romantic feelings for Peter, and they decide to inform Teddy of her intention to leave him for Peter.

But events interfere, and twice she postpones telling her husband. As she does so, Rattigan convincingly suggests that she is weakening in her resolve. Unable previously to verbalize his feelings for her or demonstrate his love, Teddy finally finds opportunity to do so when after a series of harrowing bombing missions, Patricia has been informed by his loyal men of his solid sterling English qualities. In a decision reminiscent of Shaw's Candida, who finally chooses her minister-husband, Morrell, over the young poet, Marchbanks, Patricia decides to remain with Teddy. Her choice is not an easy one, for he is not romantic as is Peter. Hers is a practical choice, dictated by Teddy's need for her. It is the hard choice that most of Rattigan's characters make, rather than one that would make for a happy, romantic ending. In addition to giving up Peter, Patricia, for the moment at least, gives up her next stage role in London. Criticized by some for its melodramatic banality, this main plot contains a Chekhovian indeterminateness and sadness that accompany the romantically unfulfilled marriage. Chekhov's women eventually have to settle for dull schoolmasters or clerks rather than dashing officers or romantic writers. So Patricia quietly makes her decision not to leave Teddy for the more romantically fulfilling life with Peter in the theater.

Although Patricia and Teddy are the main romantic interest in the plot, other characters garnered the praise of the reviewers. Particularly colorful, sympathetic, and sad is Doris, the ex-cockney barmaid, now wife of an aristocratic Polish airman whose wife and children had been killed by the Nazis. By means of an old, well-made play device, eavesdropping, we learn that underneath her gay exterior she has been living with the fear that Count Skriczevinsky will cast her off after the war. If Patricia and Teddy are mismatched romantically, Doris and her count are certainly cultural mismatches. Her outward gaiety and her drinking are disguises for her fears, and she reminds us of Masha in Chekhov's *The Seagull,* who is in mourning for her life and so drinks and wears black.

A third couple, Sergeant (Dusty) Miller and his wife, a laundry worker, provide a rich vein of humor as misunderstandings about bus times and routes provide comic relief from the tensions of the bombing missions.

Other characters (including the landlady, the boy-waiter, and a variety of military personnel—all bound by a common cause symbolized by the flare path lights that guide departing and returning bombers in their missions) develop strong ties. Intense laughter and tears of wartime life are shared by all except the outsider, Peter.

The *New Statesman* reviewer Roger Marvell wrote that the "variety of these figures and their relationships are brilliantly silhouetted; the alternations of fear and relief are highly dramatic, but tactfully interwoven with the comedy of character."[3] The main plot, he argues, is less successful than the lesser ones because the actor is never developed to gain any sympathy, perhaps by overwriting of his normally excellent naturalistic dialogue.[4] Like the *New Statesman* reviewer just quoted, Lewis Nichols of the *New York Times* regarded Rattigan at his best in the depiction of the minor characters.[5] W. A. Darlington strongly applauded Rattigan's quintessential strength, the creation of believable and entertaining characters:

Obviously this is a story which any competent hack could have thought of in a story conference in any studio of Elstree or Hollywood. However, Rattigan is not a competent hack but a real dramatist. Not only does he bring Patricia and her two men to life, but he surrounds them with vivid characters.[6]

What all the reviewers caught in their assessments was Rattigan's fascination with characters who come to life in all the significantly trivial habits of speech, manner, and gesture which define each as a memorable stage creation, reflecting the author's keen eye for the minutest and subtlest detail. The result is a character who is unique and at the same time universal. It is this end that is served by the narrative and by whatever melodramatic element may be there. The realism of character is strong enough to keep genuine sentiment from slipping into sentimentality or mawkishness. It is, as Darlington has aptly put it, the difference between a Hollywood or Elstree hack and a *real* dramatist.

Like *French Without Tears*, *Flare Path* is constructed in small, cameolike scenes, each of which is a masterfully complete dramatic unit. The rapidity of the scenes, rather than the sketchy plot, and the smiling sadness of the realistic characters, rather than superficially romantic people, create the unifying mood of the drama. The unity is further tightened by the framework device, the common cause of World War II, a cause in which all the characters except Peter participate, regardless of class. There are no villains and no heroes. There is, perhaps, not even the conventional "leading" role.

The overall pattern of the play is contained in the shape of each act. Patricia's delay in informing Teddy of impending separation at the end of Act I takes on a more definite cast at the conclusion of Act II when Peter

watches Patricia and Teddy as they go up the stairs to their bedroom. And
the third act concludes with Patricia's decision to remain with Teddy.
Rattigan's well-crafted act construction moves Patricia from her romantic
insistence on self-satisfaction to the necessary interdependence of the
wartime situation. In another situation, the ending could be considerably
different. In any event, character and plot are seamed tightly by the
demands of the time. Patricia tells Peter that their "private happiness was
something far too important to be affected by outside things, like the war
or marriage vows."[7] Now, however, she finds herself feeling like a coward.
"It may be just my bad luck, but I've suddenly found that I'm in that
battle, and I can't . . . desert."[8] Events have moved her to her decision,
and that movement is seen in the endings of each of the three acts.

By 1942, familiar concerns of Rattigan's are forming a pattern of sorts: a
foreign language is being taught the Polish count by his wife, providing
much humor; a small dash of aristocracy—here Polish—adds the exotic
and heroic touch as well; the close fraternity among males finds a most
natural context in war; at the same time the women characters are strong
and fascinating; ill-matched marriages are the rule: Patricia and Teddy,
Dusty and Maudie, Doris and her count. All three women, different as
their backgrounds are, bear their romantic frustrations with the fortitude
and pain so characteristic of English tradition. The difference between a
world in which one merely survives and a life lived fully is ironically
expressed by Peter to Patricia.

Five little bits of paper dumped on my bed with my morning tea, and you expect
me to jump on the first train up to London and fade quietly out of your life
muttering, "It's a far, far better thing"—(*Bitterly.*) Who's living in a film world,
you or me?[9]

Rattigan avoids the only too possible maudlinism by the understanding of
themselves which his characters possess. What he realizes in *Flare Path* is a
sure, steady, and full characterization by means of individual scenes and
narrative art, an achievement that in later plays like *Separate Tables*
produced mid-twentieth-century characters unrivaled on the English
stage until the appearance of Jimmy Porter.

While the Sun Shines: A Farce

Rattigan's second World War II stage play broke existing records with
its 1,154 performances. A complexly plotted farce of exaggerated and

highly improbable events, *While the Sun Shines,* 1943, follows his serious drama, *Flare Path,* in a pattern of balancing a serious play with a comedy that he maintained through most of his career.

Considered by some reviewers to be his best farce, *While the Sun Shines* illustrates Rattigan's skill in adroitly maneuvering well-timed exits and entrances to produce a complicated series of misunderstandings and the consequent hilarity and happy ending. The setting is the Albany chambers on Piccadilly where Rattigan himself lived on several occasions. Within a space of twenty-four hours young Lord Harpenden brings to his chambers an intoxicated American serviceman; his fiancée, Elizabeth, brings a French officer whom she has met on the train trip in; and Elizabeth's penniless, titled uncle appears to further complicate matters. Mulvaney has been bounced from a bar for unruly conduct and rescued by Harpenden. At the time, Harpenden, an unsuccessful matelot (*gob* to his American counterpart), has managed a short leave for his wedding to Elizabeth, an intelligent, upper-class member of the Women's Air Force. En route to her wedding festivities, she is impressed by the French officer, Colbert, whose Gallic eloquence persuades her that she needs to marry someone who will cause a "white-hot burning passion of the heart."[10]

Mistaking her for Harpenden's mistress, Mabel Crum, Mulvaney makes love to her after both have become intoxicated. The act ends with the three servicemen—British, American, and French—rolling dice for the first chance to speak to Elizabeth on the telephone. All three are gentlemanly in their respectively national and social ways, and after the misunderstandings have been cleared and the romantic entanglements straightened, Elizabeth will marry Harpenden. The play ends with another dice game, this time to determine whether Mulvaney or Colbert will be best man at Elizabeth's wedding to Harpenden.

The situation recalls the three men—Kit, Rogers, Alan—of *French Without Tears* and their involvements with the seductress, Diana. Elizabeth, however, is more than a seductress. She is eminently sensible, and her flirtation with Mulvaney, during which she experiences the white-hot passion spoken of by Colbert, only convinces her of her affection for Harpenden, Bobby to his friends. The long series of events based on misunderstandings entertained audiences for the record-breaking run of the play. The farcical encounters so successfully drawn in the earlier *First Episode* and *French Without Tears* sparkle with the polish and sophistication that come only with seasoned skills.

While the play was referred to as an adroit farce which "vanished leaving hardly a trace in the memory,"[11] the familiar Rattigan themes and stylistic qualities are fresh. Foreigners and foreign languages create much humor, as in the phrase *arrière pensée,* confused by Mabel Crum for *derrière pensée.* Rattigan used again the language misunderstanding of the opening scene of *French Without Tears,* which had evoked an explosion of laughter that continued throughout the play. The situational farce is compelling, as in the scene in which the Duke, Lord Harpenden, Colbert, and Mulvaney are playing "craps," taught by the American.

Among the themes Rattigan continues in this World War II farce is that of close male relationships that develop, even with the nationalistic differences represented in the group. And there are the two kinds of women, like Diana and Jacqueline of *French Without Tears* and like Lady Hamilton and Lady Nelson in the much later Nelson play. One is physically attractive and romantically irresistible, and the other is sensible, strong-willed, virtuous. Patricia in *Flare Path* is a combination of the two, although very seldom in a Rattigan play do the two types converge in one woman. Elizabeth is also such a woman.

Rattigan's lifelong interest in foreign languages and foreigners pervades the characters and plots of his plays. While foreigners, especially Americans, are the source of humor and satire, he does not allow them to develop into caricatures. The Irish-American Mulvaney conducts himself as naturally as do the aristocratic Harpenden and the sophisticated Colbert. Nowhere is he humiliated or even embarrassed. Indeed, he is the character through whose actions the complications arise and the means by which Elizabeth is finally educated into the right reasons for marrying Harpenden, to whom she is so practically suited, as was Patricia in *Flare Path* to the unromantic Teddy.

Even more serious themes of Rattigan are explicitly present in the lively debates with their exchange of national customs, attitudes, and language. Harpenden is told by Colbert that his social class is doomed to extinction, and Elizabeth, with her British fortitude, agrees to meet that doom with him. The colorful vitality of Mulvaney's American slang and the humor of Colbert's malapropisms are handled with ease, so that underneath the incongruities and improbabilities of the plot, there is a witty exchange of attitudes. The exchange between Harpenden and Colbert about the British upper classes contains Shavian overtones.

> Colbert: The world is no longer what it was when this match between you and Elizabeth was first planned. Les droits de seigneur have gone—never to return. You are a doomed class.

Harpenden: All right. I'm a doomed class, but that's no reason I shouldn't
                 marry the girl I love, is it?
Colbert: Certainly it is, when that girl is Elizabeth. At all costs she must
                 be saved from sharing your doom.
Harpenden: Left wing, eh?
Colbert: Socialiste.
Harpenden: Well, I read the *New Statesman* myself.
Colbert: That will not save you from extinction.[12]

Notwithstanding his quarrel with Shaw in the *New Statesman* about the
place of ideas in drama, Rattigan does engage his characters in lively
debates like that just quoted, but the ideas are neither central nor
gratuitous to the characters. Restating this point in advice to young
writers, he insisted on writing what he *wanted* to write, not what he *ought*
to write. "A theatre is a place for laughter and tears, a temple of emotion,
not of the intellect. I prefer to do my thinking in the library. What I want
to bring to the theatre is my emotion."[13] Yet, Harpenden and Colbert,
educated and literate, do express ideas, but as a natural consequence of
their natures rather than as authorial attitudes.

While the Sun Shines is a temple of laughter. The London *Times* reviewer
noted that "Mr. Rattigan's new play successfully exercises the privilege of
farce in squaring restricting reality with the lawless dream."[14] "Mr.
Anthony Asquith's direction is firm and lively. In short, Mr. Rattigan is
well served once more, and once more deserves to be."[15] The *Theatre Arts*
critic acknowledged "a diverting first act" which "then proceeds to
dwindle into innocuous platitudes, having at no point really made up its
mind whether it was aiming at farce or comedy."[16] Lewis Nichols of the
New York Times asserted that if Rattigan "never got around to making a
complete job on the third act . . . it is pleasant to hear laughter in the
theatre again. . . ."[17]

Again, the criticism that the farce does not maintain its level or develop
to the end of the play ignores Rattigan's stated intent to build scenes in the
Chekhov manner rather than in traditional constructions. The last act
seems, perhaps, to be anticlimactic. But both of Rattigan's early successful
comedies elude strict designations of comedy or farce. His scene construction is his way of including serious romantic interests and ideas which,
while not overriding, do take away from the purely comical quality and
provide, instead, a serious, sometimes disconcerting tone. Rattigan himself ironically recalled the criticism of Agate, who liked *While the Sun
Shines,* even though he admitted that it was patterned on *French Without*

Tears, which earlier he had called a "nothing." In a 1953 preface Rattigan described both comedies as "two products of my earlier, over-Aunt-Edna-conscious self."[18] Undisturbed by labels and "serious" critics, both plays enjoyed long runs.

Love in Idleness or *O Mistress Mine:* A Romance

Rattigan's third success in three consecutive years veered into still another dramatic mode in *Love in Idleness* (1944). Praised by critics for the performances of Alfred Lunt and Lynne Fontanne, it enjoyed considerable success abroad, as had *French Without Tears.* In the United States, where it was retitled *O Mistress Mine,* and where critics echoed those in London, audiences loved it. The Lunts took it on tour after 452 performances on Broadway, their longest stand in any play in New York. The mode of *Love in Idleness* is romance, contrasting with the seriousness of *Flare Path* and the farce of *While the Sun Shines.*

Like its two predecessors, the romance is rooted in a World War II ambience, although its plot does not directly involve events of the time except in a peripheral manner. Its emphasis is a domestic one, and the central characters are a middle-aged couple living together without benefit of clergy. Olivia Brown is a widow who, while her young son is in school in Canada, has fallen in love with Sir John Fletcher, a Cabinet Minister in charge of new tanks. When her son returns to England, she is living with Sir John. Until he is granted a divorce, Olivia's politically liberal son, Michael, is morally priggish about his mother's living in sin. The play, as Desmond McCarthy suggested in his review, could have been written as a *Sons and Lovers,* but the author did not choose this theme. If he has made young Michael "too much of the rude young ass," so that the audience "has no reason to suspect that he could be dearer to her than her lover,"[19] it is what Rattigan intended, even though the consequent tension between the two is not as credible as it may be. Again the critics seemed to be disconcerted by the mixture, this time of serious romance and comedy with all the problems of a domestic drama. But it is the tension within Olivia rather than explained motivation that is built up, beginning with the Hamlet-like scene in which Michael buries his head in his mother's lap. She allows the son to resolve the problem when he has his own experiences of the heart, having gained thereby some understanding of the relationship between his mother and Sir John.

This understanding Rattigan manages deftly by the age-old device of reversal, illustrated in the final act by Michael's adopting the habits he had previously scorned as capitalistic and upper class in Sir John, habits such as dinner at the Savoy, the use of cologne, and a more comfortable flat than the one he and his mother had occupied in Baron's Court, a seedy London area. The change is credible without Rattigan's providing explanations for it. The age and actions of the youth are sufficient reason.

Another time-honored device, the play-within-a-play, becomes a technique for the reversal of young Michael's attitude. In Act I Olivia rehearses with Sir John the scene in which she will have to tell Michael of her domestic arrangements. The euphemistic language and white lies she invents do not meet with his approval, and although she agrees to discard this playacting, she is reluctant and embarrassed to tell Michael the complete truth, so, of course, he eventually finds out for himself.

Similarly, Michael in Act II engages in acting out his Hamlet-like role. He reads a book on poison; he talks about seeing a play, *Murder in the Family*; he wears a black tie on the evening his mother is giving a party. Although he is serious and although at this point Sir John regards the antic disposition seriously, the histrionics are amusing.

Still a third interior play emerges in Act III when the son, having matured somewhat, rehearses with Sir John the scene they will enact that evening at the Savoy when they will attempt to impress Michael's actress friend Sylvia, who will be dining there with Michael's rival for her affections. The act concludes with Olivia's discovery of the rehearsal and the departure of all three for the Savoy. The drama is not wholly a romance or a comedy or a problem play. The style is comic but the subject is serious in its themes of parent-child relationships, hypocrisy of attitudes toward unhappy marriages, and the collapse of ideological stances under the impact of deep human relationships. There is even a brief reference to Lord Nelson and Lady Hamilton, about whom Rattigan later wrote a television play, a stage drama, and a film script. The mixture of contemporary concerns and selected conventional stylistic devices is Rattigan's consistent, if disconcerting, pattern of writing.

W. A. Darlington refers to the general reluctance of the "London dramatic critics to commit themselves about the merits of *Love in Idleness*. . . . Irving [producer] wanted a vehicle for his personal gift of freezing the marrow in men's bones; the Lunts want a vehicle for their gift of melting men's hearts with the spectacle of a human relationship."[20] And American critics again echoed their British counterparts: ". . . they [the Lunts] return to the type of elegant farce-comedy which they have earmarked as their own. They play it well, if not better than ever; which does not mean that they need play it forever."[21] But audiences loved the play and the Lunts in London and New York.

The charm of the play was agreed to by most critics even while they generally dismissed it as a trifle. Yet although labeling it a trifle, critics aimed comments at its serious content. The moral indignation of Brooks Atkinson, for example, seems incredible today. "Although the lives of thousands of soldiers depend upon the correct construction of tanks, Mr. Rattigan keeps on chattering about tanks with infinite jest as though they were of no more consequence than convertible roadsters."[22] He further accuses Rattigan of being unable to distinguish between what is real and what is not real, because the young son is bought off "with a handful of banknotes as though this solved everything."[23] Because the son, who espoused liberal attitudes, does not come off favorably, the play is "tone deaf and insensitive."[24] Overlooked in this comment is Rattigan's honesty toward his characters, even when they do not conform to behavioral standards that would seem commensurate with their ideological stances. His sympathetic sensitivity to the intimate romantic and domestic realities transcends ideological views, even his own.

Love in Idleness is a romantic drama in which he explores the plight of the woman who must explain to her young son her domestic and romantic liaison with a man to whom she is not married. She is the first fully developed character among his women to claim kinship to the women in the plays of Chekhov and Tennessee Williams. Although she is more poignantly realized as a character in later plays, for a romantic comedy her realization is more than sufficient.

Olivia's comment at the conclusion of Act II, when she is told that the Randalls who were rehearsing for a new comedy would be late for her party, expresses Rattigan's continued insistence on the purpose of his plays: "I do think that in times like these it's far better to make people laugh than to make them cry."[25] And his own oft-repeated sentiment and conviction supports Olivia's: "I rejoice in the death . . . of the cult of the play of ideas and the re-emergence since the war, in Europe as in America, of the play that unashamedly says nothing except possibly that human beings are strange creatures, and worth putting on the stage where they can be laughed at or cried over, as our pleasure takes us."[26] His justification for his stage people is amply realized in the trilogy of World War II plays of the early 1940s. The people caught in the events and moods of the period continue to reflect the themes of the 1930 dramas, although here historical events shape and determine their lives more sharply than in earlier plays.

Chapter Seven
Serious Recognition: *The Winslow Boy*

By 1944 Rattigan had to his credit nine plays: four were unqualified stage successes, four for various reasons evoked moderate to favorable responses, and one remains unproduced on the London stage. Then, Rattigan explained, the idea for *The Winslow Boy* which "had so fascinated and moved me . . . unlike many ideas that will peacefully wait in the store-room of the mind until their time for emergence has come . . . demanded instant expression."[1]

Based on the famous Archer Shee case of 1908 in which a family fought for nearly two years to vindicate their young son, their family honor, and "what is right," the drama produced in 1946 was his first clearly critical and popular success. An Osborne naval cadet, young Archer Shee, was dismissed upon being accused of stealing a five-shilling postal order from a fellow cadet's locker. The famous barrister Edward Carson successfully defended the boy in a protracted suit that attracted the attention of a whole nation in a time when vaster national concerns, according to some individuals and newspapers, merited public attention. The play received the Ellen Terry Award (the first of two) as the best of the 1946 London season.

A Drama of Character

The first of Rattigan's published plays in four acts, the drama, like the real-life trial, spans two years. In four acts, Rattigan plausibly and adroitly maneuvers the melodramatic plot toward in-depth characterizations which both subdue the potential sensationalism and temper the potential sentimentality of an already highly dramatic and emotional subject. The emphasis in the play is not the schoolboy, young Ronnie Winslow, as the

57

title suggests, nor is it the principle of right, even when the defense of that principle involves fighting the highest court of the land in the defense of a single individual. It is not even the dramatic excitement of the court trial that holds the reader's attention as it moves toward the vindication of Ronnie Winslow. Important as these three elements may be, they are only the means by which Rattigan has developed for the first time characters who, in spite of the melodramatic qualities of their situation, are not only credible but memorable.

Although Ronnie appears in the strong confrontations with his father and then with Sir Robert Morton at the conclusions of Acts I and II—cliff hangers in the well-made-play tradition and also indicators of the play's conclusion—he remains a boy visibly untouched by the events. Through the rest of the play he appears only occasionally. In fact, in Act IV, when the verdict of the trial is reported, Ronnie is at the movies. Also, during the two years in which the events of the case transpire, he has been attending another school quite uneventfully.

As emphasis on the boy diminishes, that on his father, sister, and lawyer increases, since it is they who make the sacrifices necessary to the defense of what is right. The father withdraws his older son from Oxford, and the family suffers financial strictures in order to pursue their cause. Then when the cause seems lost and they even consider withdrawing the suit, it is Sir Robert who persuades them to continue. Catherine suffers a broken engagement to an attractive young man whose concern for his family reputation causes withdrawal of his engagement to her. She reconsiders, although not conclusively, the long-standing suit of a family counselor who stands by the family during their ordeal. Strong-willed and practical, she is a woman in the Pankhurst tradition, a liberated woman upon whom her father leans heavily, especially when his health fails.

Finally, Sir Robert, although not suffering, gives up an offer to become Lord Chief Justice "in order to be able to carry on with the case of Winslow versus Rex." Subtly emerging in Rattigan's portrayal of Ronnie's defense lawyer is the revelation of his real passion underneath the facades of cold logic, histrionic style, and his distant—in Catherine's words, "fishy"—manner. For Sir Robert cries when the verdict is announced, and in the final scene in which Catherine is cross-examining him, he hopes that perhaps he will someday see Catherine in the gallery of the House of Commons, not "across the floor." Ronnie appears only briefly in this last scene to thank Sir Robert. But it is Arthur, Catherine, and Sir Robert who emerge as strongly developed characters.

Characterization by Scene Construction

As in *First Episode,* focus gradually shifts in successive acts and in scenes within acts from Ronnie to Arthur, Catherine, and, finally, Sir Robert. So what appears to be a shift of focus is not a matter of weak plot construction. It is, rather, a deliberately progressive revelation of the characters, all of whom reflect in different ways and to varying degrees the values of the father, Arthur Winslow.

Even minor characters have individual strong scenes in which their traditional English fortitude and fair play reinforce those of Arthur. Dickie, Ronnie's older brother, who is working in a bank in Reading, announces that he has joined the Territorials in the event that there may be a "bit of a scrap" so that he would have a "bit of a change" before he settles down to bank life, as his father had. In reality, he is hiding his disappointment at not being able to continue at university. Desmond Curry, faithful suitor of Catherine and supporter of the Winslow family, eventually earns a reconsideration of his suit with Catherine. Violet, the loyal but sometimes embarrassingly unconventional maid, stays on in spite of reduced financial arrangements. Mr. and Mrs. Winslow can look forward to a resumption of their life, even though Mr. Winslow's health has been impaired. It is by means of the courageous carrying on of normal activity in the family, a normality that has exacted its price from each member, that the melodrama is held in check and that is the very basis for Rattigan's scene construction. Although the scenes themselves may remind one more of Shaw than of Chekhov, in their rapid-fire dialogues, their purpose, like that of Chekhov, is to develop character.

As a drama in which scenes and plot are so clearly used in the service of characterization, structure here deserves some comment. In the Scribean, formulaic well-made play, the first act is usually devoted to a long, creaky explication of character and situation. Action in Rattigan's first act begins immediately as Ronnie Winslow, cold and wet, stealthily arrives home from Osborne. Although the conventional maid is the first to welcome him, it is not long until he faces the family and confronts his father in the crisply handled confrontation with which Act I concludes.

Ronnie's arrival coincides with a family event in which John Watherstone arranges with Arthur Winslow the financial details of his impending marriage to Catherine. In the course of this event, the liberal attitudes and warm relationships of the family are established, and the strong-mindedness of Catherine emerges as she discusses John with her mother and as she reflects on the manner in which she will break the engagement news to her long-standing suitor, Desmond Curry. Reminiscent of the educated, liberated Mary of O'Casey's *Juno and the Paycock* and of Mrs. Alving in Ibsen's *Ghosts,* Catherine talks about her reading of radical literature. Arthur, who has been listening to the conversation, chuckles at his daughter's exchange with her mother. In the ease with which he discusses matters with her, it is obvious that he and she are cut from the same cloth. Not surprisingly, then, Catherine develops into a female counterpart of her father. And with family support and her as yet unentangled life, she seems able to survive the disappointment when John eventually decides to marry someone else.

In the scene between Catherine and her mother, there is a crispness of dialogue that resembles the tension of a courtroom examination. It anticipates the brilliant scene of Ronnie with Arthur at the end of Act I, the electrifying scene of Ronnie with Sir Robert at the conclusion of Act II, and, finally, the subdued challenges between Catherine and Sir Robert at the end of Act IV.

Unconventional Climaxes

One of the unique aspects of the play's construction is the omission of actual courtroom scenes. In a departure from convention, the events of the trial are reported from time to time by various family members. The most effective of these reports is made by Violet, longtime maid of the family, who literally steals the stage with her highly emotional announcement of the verdict and the reaction of the public to that verdict. Her long monologue carries with it all the exultation which the real case of Archer Shee brought to a nation caught up in the drama of the trial. In putting the external climax of the play into a monologue by a maid, Rattigan veers from well-made-play tradition, which would have made dramatic "hay" of the jury's verdict. Without the histrionics of the conventional climax, which would have involved the main characters, Rattigan's maid carries the emotional impact of a Chekhovian scene.

Yet the real or inner climax of the play is contained not in the maid's demonstrative report but in the subdued scene between Catherine and her father just prior to Violet's announcement. Here Catherine informs her father that John will be marrying another woman, and this information leads the two into an introspective analysis of their pursuit of the case at such cost. In response to Arthur's query about her possible marriage to Desmond Curry, Catherine merely replies, "In the words of the Prime

Minister, Father,—wait and see." Personal matters are subordinated to the larger and more compelling good.

Indeed, she responds with a quiet triumph to Sir Robert's challenge at the end. Asked whether he would see her in the House one day, she replies, "Yes, Sir Robert. One day. But not in the Gallery. Across the floor." Like the climaxes, Rattigan's ending of the play is not Scribean, for Catherine's future remains to be decided. Marriage to John or Desmond or a possible romance with Sir Robert is not the happy ending of this play. On the other hand, the conclusion is not the standard one of the well-made problem play of Pinero in which the woman is victimized by societal attitudes. And, unlike the alienation of Ibsen's Mrs. Alving or Hedda Gabler, Catherine is confirmed in her sacrifice by her family and society. In succeeding plays by Rattigan, the self-realization by characters will be more painful and costly than Catherine's here. Similarly, the scenes, acts, climaxes, and conclusions will follow the pattern realized in *The Winslow Boy*.

Significance of Rattigan's First Major Critical Success

What he began in *First Episode,* deepened in *After the Dance* and *Flare Path,* Rattigan has sophisticated in *The Winslow Boy.* The narrative progresses not by artificial plotting but by the strong beliefs and emotions that each character brings to his actions and by the common bond of the situation in which the characters find themselves. The common cause may be undergraduate ties, wartime events, or the fight of the little man against the highest court in the land. But individuals within that cause are of primary value, and each person is effectively developed in the strong scenes constructed with an ease not evident in the earlier dramas. In both matured craftsmanship and in a confident handling of complex relationships among a variety of characters, *The Winslow Boy* is Rattigan's first solid achievement. The shadows cast by both the themes and style will only be lengthened in the plays yet to be discussed.

Chapter Eight

Playbill: The Browning Version and Harlequinade

The Browning Version

Reinforcing the solid dramatic achievement of *The Winslow Boy,* Rattigan triumphed two years later in *The Browning Version* (1948), one of a duo of plays produced under the title *Playbill.* Like its predecessor, this drama develops from a schoolboy experience, this time a personal one involving a schoolmaster who has failed in both his marriage and profession. *The Browning Version* draws on Rattigan's acquaintance with an older classics master, Mr. Coke Norris, who taught *Agamemnon* as an exercise in translation, exhibiting emotion and humor so seldom that he was unpopular with the students. Even the gift of a book on his retirement seemed not to move him at all.[1] From this brief acquaintance, Rattigan, nearly twenty-five years later, developed a dramatic character who for many theatergoers and critics is the most moving and memorable of all his characters.

Crocker-Harris, the target of jokes by the schoolboys, his colleagues, and even his wife, has had to retire early for health reasons. On this, his penultimate day at the public school, we see him first by means of an accidental meeting between his student, Taplow, and a science master, Frank Hunter. The former arrives for an extra tutorial session and is anxious about receiving his "remove" in classics. The latter is visiting Millie Crocker-Harris, with whom he has had a desultory affair.

"The Crock's" failure as a schoolmaster emerges at once in the frank discussions between Taplow and Hunter as Rattigan clearly establishes the situation which had earned for him the title of the "Himmler of the lower fifth." The student, Taplow, has just stolen two pieces of chocolate from a box in the master's flat, eating one, and, whether from a siege of "conscience or his judgment of what he might be able to get away with,"[2] returning the other. Frank Hunter enters, and they talk about Crocker-

Harris. Worried about his passing, Taplow divulges the information that his classics master is perhaps the only faculty member who, following school rules, does not announce grades before the last day of the term. Further, he mimics the "very gentle, rather throaty voice" of Crocker-Harris: ". . . I have given you exactly what you deserve. No less; and certainly no more." Hunter assures Taplow that his remove will be granted "for being a good boy in taking extra work," whereupon the student responds, "Well, I'm not so sure, sir. That would be true of the ordinary masters, all right. They just wouldn't dare not give a chap a remove after his taking extra work—it would be such a bad advertisement for them. But those sort of rules don't apply to the Crock—Mr. Crocker-Harris."[3]

Taplow goes on to say that he doesn't "know any boy who doesn't trade on that very foible."[4] Hunter's way with the students is obviously easy; he establishes rapport immediately with Taplow by discussing his golf swing, and he freely admits to the student that he's not interested in the science that he has to teach. Rather, Hunter is more interested in being liked by the schoolboys, and he succeeds in his attempts. Crocker-Harris's intended jokes—puns on Greek words—evidently are lost on the boys. With the years, the failure to be popular has only resulted in his becoming an object of mimicry. To Gilbert, his replacement, who unwittingly hurt Crocker-Harris by revealing his nickname, Himmler of the lower fifth, the master said: "I knew, of course, that I was not only not liked, but now positively disliked. I had realized, too, that the boys—for many long years now—had ceased to laugh at me. I don't know why they no longer found me a joke. Perhaps it was my illness. No, I don't think it was that. Something deeper than that. Not a sickness of the body, but a sickness of the soul. At all events it didn't take much discernment on my part to re-alize I had become an utter failure as a schoolmaster. Still, stupidly enough, I hadn't realized that I was also feared. The Himmler of the lower fifth! I suppose that will become my epitaph."[5]

Later in the play Crocker-Harris admits that he had known of his failure but that facing it is the most difficult part; he also faces his marital failure when he informs Hunter not only that he had known of his wife's affair with the science master, but that she herself had told him. Almost simultaneously, Hunter develops a sympathy for Crocker-Harris, a bond first revealed in his conversation with Taplow and later in the scene in which Millie taunts her husband with deliberate cruelty. With Hunter and Gilbert, Crocker-Harris's admission of his failure is explicit. But with Taplow, where the emotion is so much stronger than words, the experience is handled by Rattigan in subtextual fashion that recalls the obliqueness of

Chekhov. Crocker-Harris has just told Taplow that *Agamemnon* is "perhaps
the greatest play ever written," to which Taplow quickly replies, "I
wonder how many people in the form think that?" Although apologizing
instantly, he has with his innocent cruelty externalized for the master the
suppressed sense of failure with which he has so long lived. Crocker-Harris
"sits motionless staring at his book."[6] Unable to react directly to the
question and apology, Crocker-Harris recovers sufficiently to murmur
gently:

> When I was a very young man, only two years older than you are now,
> Taplow, I wrote, for my own pleasure, a translation of the
> *Agamemnon*—a very free translation—I remember—in rhyming
> couplets.
> Taplow. The whole *Agamemnon*—in verse? That must have been hard work,
> sir.
> Andrew. It was hard work; but I derived great joy from it. The play had so
> excited and moved me that I wished to communicate, however
> imperfectly, some of that emotion to others. When I had finished it,
> I remember, I thought it very beautiful—almost more beautiful
> than the original.
> Taplow. Was it ever published, sir?
> Andrew. No. Yesterday I looked for the manuscript while I was packing my
> papers. I was unable to find it. I fear it is lost—like so many other
> things. Lost for good.
> Taplow. Hard luck, sir.[7]

And the lesson continued in its usual humdrum manner. But for a rare,
brief moment, a spark of communication and emotion had been lit
between master and student, the first of a number which Crocker-Harris,
after so many years of suppression, is to experience in one day. And
Taplow, particularly, succeeds in understanding him, even defending him
earlier against other students' misunderstandings and insisting that "the
Crock" was not a sadist like one or two of the others. Then when Taplow
returns with a gift, a used copy of Browning's version of *Agamemnon,* with
the Greek inscription, Andrew has difficulty in speaking:

> Taplow, would you be good enough to take that bottle of medicine,
> which you so kindly brought in, and pour me out one dose in a glass
> which you will find in the bathroom?
> Andrew, *the moment he is gone, breaks down and begins to sob uncontrollably. He makes
> a desperate attempt, after a moment, to control himself, but when Taplow comes back his
> emotion is still very apparent.*

Andrew.   (*Taking the glass*) Thank-you. (*He drinks it, turning his back on Taplow as he does so. At length.*) You must forgive this exhibition of weakness, Taplow. The truth is I have been going through rather a strain lately.
Taplow.   Of course, sir. I quite understand.[8]

Crocker-Harris's embarrassing display of emotion and his even more embarrassing attempt to hide it are soon covered by his comment to Hunter, who has just returned, a comment that reinforces his earlier confession to Gilbert about the small success that can atone for a large failure:

> I am not a very emotional person, as you know, but there was something so very touching and kindly about his action, and coming as it did just after—(*He stops, then glances at the book in his hand*) This is a very delightful thing to have, don't you think?
> Frank.   Delightful.[9]

Following rapidly on the heels of this high emotional moment, Millie enters with her brutally cruel taunt of the gift as a "few bobs' worth of appeasement,"[10] and Crocker-Harris's brief "high" is shatteringly destroyed. He exits with his glass and heart medicine in hand.

What follows this climax is the kind of ending which is Rattigan's own and, again, one which bears a closer resemblance to Chekhov's than to that of the conventionally well-made playwrights. Hunter breaks off with Millie as he has been trying unsuccessfully to do in a more indirect fashion for some time. Also partly out of a strong, developed sympathy for Crocker-Harris, he insists on visiting him after he has settled in his new position at a crammer's school. Crocker-Harris in quite unmelodramatic and unemotional manner informs Millie that he will not go with her to her father's, prior to his taking the new teaching assignment. And in a growing sense of freedom, he calls the headmaster to inform him that he has changed his mind and will speak after Fletcher, the young and more popular retiree, for

I am of opinion that occasionally an anti-climax can be surprisingly effective. Goodbye. (*He rings off and goes and sits at table.*)
Come along, my dear. We mustn't let our dinner get cold.
Millie slowly sits and begins to serve dinner.
Curtain[11]

Crocker-Harris's failures would destroy most men, and one could argue that the Crock was destroyed by his experiences. At one point he refers to

his only outward display of emotion as "the muscular twitchings of a
corpse. It can never happen again."[12] Yet the fact that it did happen freed
him to act decisively in the final moments of the play when he chose to
follow rather than precede a popular master as speaker at the prize-giving
ceremony. A small action, the choice represents his break with the
mockery that his professional life at the school had been. And although he
has accepted a new teaching position in a less prestigious school, he will
begin with a sense of freedom gained by his defiance of the popularity
contest that teaching can deteriorate into. He also feels free from the
hypocrisy and mediocrity with which he has been surrounded, for he is the
most brilliant university graduate to have come to the school. Along with
his freedom, Crocker-Harris will take with him the newly gained sympathetic understanding of Hunter, who, realizing the shallowness and
cruelty of Millie, breaks off their liaison. Furthermore, even though
Hunter's attempt to lessen Crocker-Harris's humiliation by suggesting
that perhaps the student's gift of Browning's translation of *Agamemnon* was
not a bribe for a grade seems not to have had its intended effect, it does
enable the Crock to speak openly of what he had been enduring privately.
So, his own comment not withstanding, he is not a corpse.

In advice offered to the young schoolmaster who was to replace him,
Andrew Crocker-Harris—"the Crock" to his lower fifth form students of
the classics—offered an intimate glimpse of himself denied to his wife and
colleagues: "I can only teach you from my own experience. For two or three
years I tried very hard to communicate to the boys some of my own joy in
the great literature of the past. Of course, I failed, as you will fail, nine
hundred and ninety-nine times out of a thousand. But a single success can
atone and more than atone for all the failures in the world. And
sometimes—very rarely, it is true—but sometimes I had that success.
That was in the early years."[13]

Among the many ironies in the play—which serve to tone down
possible sentimentality—is that the farewell gift of the student is Browning's version of the *Agamemnon*, whose faultiness both student and master
admit, yet whose excitement Taplow feels. His excitement is not unlike
that once felt by Crocker-Harris about his own translation, now lost, as is
his ability to communicate his enthusiasm to the students.

Irony continues in the similarity of the marital situation of the
Crocker-Harrises to that of Agamemnon and Clytemnestra, particularly as
it is innocently evoked in Taplow's words to Hunter: "Well, no, Sir, I don't
think the play is muck—exactly. I suppose, in a way, it's rather a good
plot, really, a wife murdering her husband and having a lover and all that.

I only meant the way it's taught to us—just a lot of Greek words strung together and fifty lines if you get them wrong."[14] Crocker-Harris's personal and professional failures fuse poignantly in the schoolboy's words. Just as Agamemnon comes home from the Trojan War to Clytemnestra, who has been living with Aegisthus, so Crocker-Harris comes home from the classroom to an unfaithful wife and her lover, about whose affair the master and the whole school know. His first display of emotion in years is followed by the Clytemnestra-like blow with which Millie demolishes a rare emotional moment.

But it is, as Harold Hobson claims, Rattigan's masterful way of bringing "living beings to the highest point of dramatic tension without in any way violating the integrity of their personalities."[15] Opposing experiences form a satisfying tension, for just as the Crock's "harshness . . . suddenly was broken down by a single act of kindness,"[16] so the long deception practiced by Millie broke open to exteriorize interior realities too long endured in suppressed states. The result is Hunter's rejection of Millie and Crocker-Harris's openly admitting the mismatched nature of his and Millie's relationship, a knowledge both had lived with in a damagingly suppressed state:

You see, my dear Hunter, she is really quite as much to be pitied as I. We are both of us interesting subjects for your microscope. Both of us needing from the other something that would make life supportable for us, and neither of us able to give it. Two kinds of love. Hers and mine. Worlds apart, as I know now, though when I married her I didn't think they were incompatible. In those days I hadn't thought that her kind of love—the love she requires and which I was unable to give her—was so important that its absence would drive out the other kind of love—the kind of love that I require and which I thought, in my folly, was by far the greater part of love. I may have been, you see, Hunter, a brilliant scholar, but I was woefully ignorant of the facts of life. I know better now, of course. I know that in both of us, the love that we should have borne each other has turned to bitter hatred. That's all the problem is. Not a very unusual one, I venture to think—nor nearly as tragic as you seem to imagine. Merely the problem of an unsatisfied wife and a henpecked husband. You'll find it all over the world. It is usually, I believe, a subject for farce.[17]

The most striking difference between this play and earlier dramas by Rattigan is the strong concentration on one character. Unlike *Flare Path* and *The Winslow Boy* in which the focus shifts, all the minor characters exist in order to dramatize the failures and the one small, atoning triumph of Andrew Crocker-Harris. Indeed, he is the first in a series of characters

Rattigan developed out of the pain of suffering and humiliation, who survive beyond hope and, therefore, beyond despair, with their dignity intact.

The concentration on a central character is achieved by the overall construction of the play in which the classical unities of time, place, and action are closely observed. And like Greek drama, *The Browning Version* is a study of a man in the final days of his life at a public school. His past is revealed to the audience by a series of well-timed entrances and exits of the student, the lover, the headmaster, the Clytemnestra-like wife, and the new master. Each of these characters provides information about the past life of Crocker-Harris, so that what remains is merely the final action by the schoolmaster resulting from the revelations and from his own facing of the truth about himself.

Yet this centuries-old technique, effectively utilized by Rattigan, is mixed with a modern, flat, upper-middle class, idiomatically naturalistic dialogue which Geoff Brown describes as "measured dialogue which emerges clipped and unmonotonously monotonous. . . ."[18] The following passage suggests these qualities with language and rhythms that match the banality and cruelty that the gentle schoolmaster is incapable of, but that he has had to endure for so many years:

Millie: Andrew? Why this sudden concern for Andrew?
Frank: Because I think he's just been about as badly hurt as a human being can be; and as he's a sick man and in a rather hysterical state it might be a good plan to go and see how he is.
Millie: (*Scornfully.*) Hurt? Andrew hurt? You can't hurt Andrew. He's dead.
Frank: Why do you hate him so much, Millie?
Millie: Because he keeps me from you.
Frank: That isn't true.
Millie: Because he's not a man at all.
Frank: He's a human being.[19]

In line with Rattigan's insistence on giving the actor freedom in rendering their implicitness, these lines could be spoken melodramatically or honestly. Eric Portman in 1948 and Nigel Stock in 1973 succeeded in keeping the honesty intact. Of Stock, Brown writes that he did not "fall into the finicky theatrics which bedeviled Michael Redgrave in the 1951 film version."[20]

In fidelity to character integrity, as well as in the classically severe sequence of scenes in *The Browning Version,* Rattigan shuns sentimentality as well as theatricality, for he has kept at bay the pity one feels for a victim and gradually substitutes admiration for a contemporary middle-class antihero who lives and eventually, if in a small way, triumphs over his life of quiet desperation. Like the failed, mediocre characters of some of Browning's dramatic monologues, the Crock belongs to a long tradition of modest, modern heroes.

Harlequinade

The lesser of the two plays presented in 1948 under the title of *Playbill*, *Harlequinade* is a farce about a road company rehearsal of *Romeo and Juliet*. W. A. Darlington described it as "an average example of Rattigan's lightest and slightest work."[21] In contrast with the very strong notices of *The Browning Version*, the play received minimal notices, in spite of its being "deftly written and delicately acted by Eric Portman, Mary Ellis and a good company."[22]

As in his earlier farces, there are the recognizable qualities of the loose plot and the seeming shifting of focus. No one character emerges strongly in this assemblage of characters out of life on both sides of the theater curtain. The main storyline involves the aging Arthur and Edna Selby Gosport, a famous acting couple, playing Romeo and Juliet, roles which create problems of lighting for them. The staging problems are complicated by intrusions from real life in the person of Muriel Palmer, who appears unexpectedly with her husband and baby. As it turns out, Gosport, in an earlier appearance in the town, had enjoyed a liaison with a local woman whom he left shortly thereafter and who, unknown to him, bore his child. After a series of hurried calls to his managers in London, the matter of possible bigamy is satisfactorily resolved for all. Just as the resolution is announced and the rehearsal problems taken care of, the lights on the stage are turned on, and Burton, the manager, frantically announces: "Take those lights out! It's seven-thirty. There's an audience in front. Look!"[23]

In the minor storylines of the play the theater and life are entangled with each other. There is Dame Maud, who once played Juliet to Arthur's father's Romeo and who persistently offers outdated advice on acting matters. And there is Jack Wakefield, stage manager, beset with his own romantic problems. His visiting fiancée is adamant about his leaving the company of actors. They part when he refuses. In the midst of the confusion of rehearsal and personal problems, George Chudleigh, playing a halberdier with one line, "Faith, we may put up our pipes and begone," resigns because he is not given the respect he wishes. His replacement runs on stage at regular intervals, sometimes off cue, vainly attempting to read his line effectively. It is the line, by now well known, with which Rattigan himself had difficulty in an Oxford production of the play during his undergraduate days.

Throughout, Edna Selby complains about harsh lights, and Dame Maud is reminded that she has not kept up with changing theatrical tastes and techniques. She is told that "the theatre of today has at last acquired a social conscience, and a social purpose. Why else do you think we're opening at this rathole of a theatre instead of the Opera House, Manchester?"[24] The stage manager has his own explanation of the theater: "As far as I can see it means playing Shakespeare to audiences who'd rather go to the films; while audiences who'd rather go to Shakespeare are driven to the films because they haven't got Shakespeare to go to. It's all got something to do with the new Britain and apparently it's an absolutely splendid idea."[25]

Discussions of the state of the theater, intrusions from real life, and stage problems of various sorts are adroitly mixed with rehearsal scenes to provide, as the London *Times* reviewer said of *First Episode*, "something for everyone." This mixture of theater and life at first suggests Pirandello's *Six Characters in Search of an Author*, but Rattigan does not dramatize the psychological confusions of illusions and reality as does Pirandello. Rattigan's concern is with a comic-realistic presentation of theatrical life.

Rattigan's masterful control of scenes in both plays of *Playbill* is evident in their final episodes. In *The Browning Version* the Crock rises to his triumph as he informs the headmaster that he prefers to follow rather than precede a popular speaker, asserting that "occasionally an anti-climax can be surprisingly effective."[26] The announcement follows his decision to break with Millie since neither of them "has the right to expect anything further from the other."[27] In *Harlequinade* the disclosure that it is 7:30 and that an audience is waiting produces a similarly antitheatrical effect, but in both cases the effect does not violate the integrity of the characters or the plot.

Rather, it conveys the occasionally brutal, always honest, psychological truths of Rattigan's characters, holding and moving audiences by steering "his dramatic craft adroitly between the nets of artifice and the shallows of sentimentality."[28]

Chapter Nine
Plays of Disillusionment

Rattigan regarded the five plays in Volume 2 of his *Collected Plays* as "in general, the history of my struggle, unsuccessful as it may well have been, to curb and control the purely 'audience' side of my creator's split mind, and thereby to transform my sense of theatre into a sense of drama."[1] Referring to his reputation "with the critics and the public alike, of being a fairly skillful exponent of good theatre," he stated that he didn't think that "anyone considered, up to and including the time of *The Winslow Boy*, that I had, or ever would have, the smallest right to call myself, in the severely critical sense of the term, a dramatist."[2] Very likely he had in mind the criticism of critics whom Kenneth Tynan quoted as saying of Rattigan's plays: "Good theatre, but. . . ." "Yet," Tynan wrote, "the deceptive ease of his success has put many of his critics on the defensive."[3] The defensiveness in both Rattigan and his critics developed into a habit, particularly during the years when popular success gained for him a reputation as a one-man theatrical establishment. Yet in the midst of the success, Rattigan worked hardest, as he put it, to "transform my sense of theatre into a sense of drama." *Adventure Story*, his first venture into historical drama, plays an important role in this transformation effort.

Adventure Story

The Rattigan treatment of Alexander the Great's story begins with a prologue in which the conqueror on his deathbed is being asked to name his successor. Although there is no designation of a successor, Ptolemy thinks he heard something like "Who shall I condemn to death?"[4] The death-bed scene of Alexander at the age of thirty-two is then continued in an epilogue in which Alexander's question is repeated and answered by him: "Who shall I condemn to death? No one. This will be my last act of mercy. Let them fight it out for themselves. Goodbye then. The adventure is over and the adventurer would like to go to sleep."[5] Between prologue and epilogue, Alexander at twenty-seven begins his conquest of the world, armed with the teachings of his famous tutor, Aristotle, and with the military manual of Homer. His stated purpose is to make of the barbarians a Hellenic world, ultimately "a world state and universal peace."[6] First, however, he consults Delphi, whose Pythia tells him that "before any others, there is one conquest you must make first. . . . Know yourself, Alexander."[7] With his surrogate father, Cleitus, and his loyal staff, he sets off on his "adventure" intent on fulfilling the boast he had made to his father. In scene after strong scene of Act I, Alexander acts daringly and honorably, whether he is bandying words with the Pythia, being chivalrous to the Queen Mother of Persia, intensifying the loyalties of his officers, or even earning the admiration of his enemies.

The drama is strong in Act I as we see Alexander in action on the military front and in personal relationships with friends, particularly his gentle relations with the Queen Mother. In Act II the action gives way to introspection as Alexander attempts to analyze himself and his actions, asking on his deathbed, "Where did it all go wrong?" Again, as in earlier plays there is the sense of dispersal of dramatic action and tension, which seemed to some critics to be a weakness. Yet, the self-questioning is consistent with the character of Aristotle-educated Alexander and, moreover, with the "madness" and the disillusionment that take over the Alexander of Act II. Both the active and passive portions of the play firmly develop from the initial scene at Delphi and are closely contained within the self-questioning of Alexander in the prologue and epilogue.

The play's production in 1949 drew the by now familiar opposing notices. "While Alexander is conquering the world held by Darius Mr. Terence Rattigan and Mr. Paul Scofield are alike at their best. It is quite extraordinary with what quiet ingenuity the author gives dramatic firmness and continuing interest to each stage of the young conqueror's progress from Babylon to Parthia; and Mr. Paul Scofield matches the strong and pointful dialogue with acting equally strong and pointful."[8] At the opposite end of the critical spectrum, the *Sunday Dispatch* critic described it much later, in 1957, as "an ambitious drama about Alexander the Great which flopped honourably in 1949."[9] The *New Statesman and Nation* fell somewhere between these ends: "His new play is not mature enough to satisfy those who have already responded emotionally to the figure of Alexander; nor, unless I am greatly mistaken, is it sufficiently crude to appeal to that large public who enjoy seeing history reduced to a sort of contemporary slip-slop."[10]

As in the case of *First Episode,* a critic then took the liberty of suggesting to Rattigan how he might have restructured the play: "He [Alexander] might be taken at the point of disillusion, after the return from India, where the whole venture could be imagined to be going sour on the conqueror . . . instead of the straightforward life of a camp soldier with its clan-like companionship where he ruled *primus inter pares,* the corruption of luxury and the necessary despotism."[11] Philip Oakes wrote in 1977 that Rattigan, after twenty-seven years, still galled about the failure of the play, wanted to do some revision on the work, which at one time he regarded as his favorite play.[12]

T. C. Worsley's review in the *New Statesman and Nation* questioned Rattigan's use of colloquial idiom and the absence of some overriding idea, and it is very likely in response to that criticism that Rattigan commented on his conscious use of language and of narrative episodes rather than ideas to express his view of Alexander's character. Shortly after the production of *Adventure Story* Rattigan wrote his article "The Play of Ideas," which began a long debate in the *New Statesman and Nation.*

Rattigan described the play as "an attempt to express, in terms of dramatic narrative, my view of the character of Alexander, and though, as my critics said at the time, it lacked the language of the poet and the perception of the philosopher, those deficiencies were both conscious and allowed for, and the attempt, I believe, was not entirely vain."[13]

The two major criticisms aimed at *Adventure Story* were the usual ones: the flat, naturalistic, idiomatic language and the diminution or dispersal of dramatic action and tension. Yet these are deliberate stylistics of Rattigan. The antiheroic language of an antiheroic age is not only a modern rendering of history; it is Rattigan's emphasis always on the human experience rather than the historical or intellectual significance of the events. T. C. Worsley argues that "if a colloquial idiom is to be used, then it must be *used*—used for the effect it can give in subordination to whatever general design there may be in some such way, for instance, as Cocteau or Anouilh use it. It cannot, except in the worst kind of film, be left to take its poor shabby little chance among the antique trapping and world-shaking events. This only makes for banality, and sometimes even for bathos."[14] Whether Rattigan's usage of banalities is banal or whether it successfully serves his general design can be determined only by the audience and the reader. The dialogue of the daring, idealistic Alexander in his encounter with the Pythia at the Oracle at Delphi can be just that: daring and idealistic. Or it risks the possibility of being handled in a fashionably flippant manner. The following passage illustrates the language usage Rattigan found himself constantly defending:

Alexander: You think I'm mad, of course.
Pythia: No. Just very young.
Alexander: All idealists are a little mad. Aristotle is madder than anyone.
Pythia: He's your tutor, isn't he?
Alexander: He was. He's gone back to Athens, now. He believes in the world
             state, too, you know.
Pythia: I see. And you're going to put his ideas into practice?
Alexander: Yes. He doesn't approve of that.
Pythia: I'm not surprised.[15]

The same idiom colors the self-analytical dialogue of the second half of the play, in which Alexander's idealism turns to tyranny and his daring to cruelty. The language throughout is of a piece, as idealism and realism cancel each other out in Alexander's final lines: "Can this really be the end? God—oh God—this is a brutal joke you are playing. The conqueror of the world dies of a chill at the age of thirty-two. How my father, Philip, must be chuckling to himself now. It doesn't matter. I've shown him, haven't I? I've shown him."[16] The cancellation is further seen in his refusal to name a successor, which he regards as his last act of mercy. As hero or tyrant, Alexander speaks in conversational idiom throughout the play.

The role of Alexander gave Paul Scofield his first major part on the London stage; later, in June 1961, Sean Connery successfully played Alexander in a favorably received BBC television presentation of the drama: "*Adventure Story* . . . presented Mr. Rattigan's work in the most favorable possible light, for whatever criticisms can be made of its reliance upon easy-going psychological explanations which sound more convincing than they really are, he builds his plays soundly, moves them along with well controlled speed, and perhaps most importantly, offers his actors the freedom to add out of their own skill and personality the intensities he does not supply in the text."[17]

One can only speculate on the effect of structural changes suggested by Worsley or of revisions projected by Rattigan himself. Perhaps as in the case of the reworking of the sexual identity of Major Pollock in the later *Separate Tables,* Rattigan would have realized that the play had already been bent into its shape and would not yield to another shape.

In particular, the critics referred to the sagging second half of the play—"when there are no more worlds to conquer and corruption sets in"[18] for Alexander—as anticlimax and as a loss of dramatic momentum. This structural dramaturgy of Rattigan's, seen as early as *First Episode* and as late as *A Bequest to the Nation,* impressed critics as a weakness, persisted for audiences as a strength, and remains a hallmark of his style. In addition, it accounts for the familiar division between critics and audiences in their responses to Rattigan's plays: "The first-night audience in St. James' Theatre gave it an enthusiastic reception last night but newspaper critics today were inclined to think Rattigan hadn't quite pulled it off. All agreed that the first half of the play, while Alexander is on the move, is excellent. . . ."[19] But in the second half "it ceases to be a play of adventure."[20]

Who Is Sylvia?

Rattigan's hallmark continues even more noticeably in *Who Is Sylvia?* (1950), a fantasy-farce about a diplomatist, "haunted since boyhood by an ideal of feminine beauty, and happily able at every stage of his brilliant career to run across some fresh . . . approximation to the ideal."[21] He lives a life in which he enjoys the best of two worlds, the conventional and the Bohemian. Each of the three acts is a playlet about another of his approximations, all of whom enjoy a physical resemblance to the sculpture of the original Sylvia in his Knightsbridge flat.

The play's action spans a thirty-three-year period. Daphne in 1917, Nora in 1929, and Doris in 1950 resemble Sylvia and are the focus of the plot in Acts I, II, and III, respectively. Lord Binfield, Mark Wright to his various amours, is an adult version of Lord Harpenden in *While the Sun Shines.* As his deceptions close in around him, the early farcical tone of the play gradually diminishes to a smiling sadness as the diplomat ages and the disparity between the ideal and the real takes on intensifying absurdity. "Humorous invention at its freshest,"[22] the first act moves into a less inventive second and finally into a repetitive third act, as age takes its toll and as Lady Binfield appears in the third act with her slightly triumphant announcement of her long-standing knowledge of his extramarital capers.

"My heroes and my villains," Rattigan wrote, "had stopped glaring at each other, boldly on the one side and malevolently on the other. They had merged gradually into one and had become much the same person. Impossibly happy endings and convenient last-act suicides had [been], or at least were in process of being, eliminated."[23] So Lady Binfield's disclosure of her knowledge of his affairs made of the farce a sad comedy. Rattigan described the play as a "genuine attempt to make a light comedy in the same style as *French Without Tears* and *While the Sun Shines*, but more adult in approach than either of those works. . . ."[24]

Like the preceding *Adventure Story*, *Who Is Sylvia?* traces the gradual disillusionment with an ideal, but in this play the subject is a diplomat. A conventional, and therefore a failed, marriage is coped with by husband and wife, and their son, who against the wishes of the father becomes an actor rather than a diplomat. When their rakish deception of the conventional world proves only an illusion, Oscar, Mark's lifetime friend and comrade in deception, asks: "What does it feel like to grow from seventeen to sixty-four in five minutes?" The final disillusionment is Caroline's (Lady Binfield) suggestion to Mark that the Sylvia with whom Mark had been in love at seventeen, now sixty-three and living in Chester Square, be invited for dinner the next week.

Although Act I is generally regarded as the freshest of the three acts, the confrontation between father and son in Act II illustrates Rattigan's scene construction at its best. Mark's son Denis has appeared unexpectedly at a party and in a scene reminiscent of *French Without Tears* confesses that he left French school at Tours, not being able to "stick it there another second." He proceeds to demonstrate for his father his failure to learn French and to announce his decision to become an actor rather than a diplomat. Comic reversal occurs as he reproaches his father for thinking of "giving up the Diplomatic. . . ." Throughout their conversation, particularly by the use of asides, Mark's "ideal"—the best of two worlds—is punctured. After Denis's questioning of Mark's leaving the diplomatic service, Oscar advises Mark: "I think, my dear chap—there's nothing for it but to prepare for an eventual evacuation."[25]

Throughout the play Oscar, a few years Mark's senior, is his constant companion and serves as a comic double, the Miles Gloriosus and Falstaffian figure of Rattigan's domestic comedy. In the early scenes of the play, Oscar is not as important a character as in later scenes, where he reinforces the empty reality which wins out over the fantasy in Mark's life. Played by Roland Culver—Mark was played by Robert Flemyng—Oscar "is much better fun as the soldier friend who faces the world and its troubles with a twinkle of spontaneous gaiety."[26] The importance of Oscar in Act III is to supply the good-humored irony needed to avoid an artificially theatrical climax. Indeed, the quasi-happy ending even in this comedy is not unlike similar endings in *The Browning Version* and *The Deep Blue Sea,* on which Rattigan said he worked hard to avoid contrived conclusions.

In this writer's opinion, Rattigan in *Who is Sylvia?* is closest to writing the serious comedy about which he so frequently spoke. In the deployment of comic devices such as a thickly plotted action moved by a series of well-timed exits and entrances and the thematic device of self-deception, *Who Is Sylvia?* is a comedy. Its ironic handling of the fantasy-reality theme, however, makes it "serious" rather than "light" comedy. The smiling sadness that deepens perceptibly in the last two acts closely resembles that tightrope between laughter and tears in a Chekhov play.

Who Is Sylvia? is a happy blending of characters and situations from Rattigan's early plays as well as from his own life. Dedicated to his father "With love, with gratitude, and in apology,"[27] the comedy has for its main character a diplomat who wants his son to follow in his footsteps, as Frank Rattigan had wished Terence to do. The son here chooses acting, as in real life the son had chosen writing. The play abounds in autobiographically drawn detail, such as Frank Rattigan's resignation from diplomatic service following a dispute with Lord Curzon; here Mark, the father, threatens to resign. Mark and his companion attended Eton; Rattigan attended Harrow. Oscar had played Lady Macbeth at Harrow, and Rattigan's flirtation with acting in *Romeo and Juliet* had already been dramatized by him in *Harlequinade.* Most important, the amorous adventures of Mark are patterned on those of Rattigan's father. One columnist reported that Rattigan's description of Mark as "slim, handsome, and witty" had appeared in the *Londoner's Diary* announcement of a new diplomatic position. Even minute details such as a guest's recognition of Mark's son, Denis, as a cricketer at Lord's, the conversations about golf between Mark and Oscar, and the mindless, cheap gossip by the young ladies about "Madam" and clothes are drawn from the world which Rattigan knew intimately.

As the pretensions of the Edwardian world of his parents, an age gone by, are exposed, the characters remain sympathetically human. But for the last time Rattigan farcically treats the privileged life to which he was born.

Now the carefree lives of the students in *French Without Tears* (1936), succeeded by the hilarious, yet sobering, antics of World War II servicemen in *While the Sun Shines* (1943), conclude in this 1950s illusion-destroying drama about aging romantics. Oxford undergraduates of the 1930s mature through wartime experience of the 1940s, and make important reassessments in 1950. The trilogy accurately chronicles the national moods of three decades of English history. Almost immediately following *Who Is Sylvia?* dramatic subject matter takes on a somber coloring for both Rattigan and the new wave of playwrights beginning to appear on the scene. For Rattigan, particularly, the interior realities of his world remain to be explored with force, compassion, and, above all, honesty, in the dramatic style he had evolved over two decades.

Generally regarded as two of his lesser plays, *Adventure Story* and *Who Is Sylvia?* appeared directly at mid-century and at the mid-point in his career. During the remaining two decades of his life, Rattigan's stage plays, except for a fantasy entitled *The Sleeping Prince*, are devoted exclusively to explorations of lonely, failed, flawed, dislocated characters from this same upper-middle class or from history.

Chapter Ten
Two Triumphs and a Trifle
The Deep Blue Sea

The recognition which greeted Rattigan's next play, *The Deep Blue Sea* (1952), must have been gratifying to him. T. C. Worsley of the *New Statesman and Nation* found the play "extremely poignant . . . concentrated, taut and true. The theme is painful and harrowing in the extreme. But Mr. Rattigan has refused the temptation to make concessions. He gives us the impression of having faced his subject as squarely as he knew how and of having brought to bear on it all the conviction of which he was capable. Consequently it bears the unmistakable stamp of sincerity; it rings right . . . through and through."[1] Even Kenneth Tynan regarded it as the play in which Rattigan "hit his full stride . . . a masterpiece of pure theatre."[2]

Perhaps more meaningful to Rattigan were the reviews of revivals of *The Deep Blue Sea* in 1971 in a Guilford production and in 1977 at the Cambridge Arts Theatre. Of the first, Michael Billington wrote "that those who see Rattigan purely as an advocate of the traditional English public school virtues are attaching the wrong stereotype to the wrong dramatist."[3] "After Christopher Fry, Terence Rattigan is probably the dramatist who suffered most from the shock waves created by the 1956 theatrical breakthrough. Only the most rigidly doctrinaire playgoer, however, could want to bury a work such as this, which combines meticulous craftsmanship with a genuine and hard-won compassion."[4] And of the 1977 revival, David Self wrote: "They say that the difference between a journeyman playwright and a great dramatist is that the latter has something to say which touches the human condition. By the happy coincidence of these two productions [the second was *Cause Célèbre*] we are given ample proof that even if Rattigan has only one message, it is still a message worth saying and one that is relevant today as it was 25 years ago."[5]

Hester Collyer, the central character in *The Deep Blue Sea,* remains one of the unforgettable names of Rattigan's dramas, for she is a total study in feminine sexual and emotional frustration. Married to a successful judge whose values and way of life are compatible with her own upbringing and for whom she has respect and deep affection, she needs more than the traditional marriage offers. In *While the Sun Shines,* Colbert described this need as a white-hot passion. Hester finds it with Freddie Page in an affair which in every other respect is incompatible with Hester's sensitive nature and her background. She has been living with Freddie Page for nearly a year, having deserted her affluent barrister-husband, Sir William Collyer. Freddie's life, as Hester herself states, stopped in 1940, and he has failed to make a success of any job he has held since the war. For him, life has been reduced to golfing with friends at Sunningdale (a golfing haven for Rattigan) and, at irregular intervals, coming home to Hester. In his limited way he loves Hester but cannot express it in any form except physical sexuality. Hester, on the other hand, identifies her obsessive need for Freddie as a feeling no one else can explain. "It's all far too big and confusing to be tied up in such a neat little parcel and labelled lust. Lust isn't the whole of life—and Freddie is, you see, to me. The whole of life—and of death, too, it seems. Put a label on that, if you can—"[6] Her overwhelming need of Freddie is encapsulated in her reactions to his lapse of memory in regard to her birthday: two attempted suicides and her final acceptance of his departure.

In the course of the many conversations with her husband and neighbors, Hester defines the confusion of her feelings and her final decision. Recounting to Sir William the events at Sunningdale during which she met Freddie, she said she "knew then in that tiny moment when we were laughing together so close that I had no hope. No hope at all."[7] Collyer then replies with a question about her belief in affinities, to which she responds, "If there are good affinities there must be evil ones too, I suppose."[8] For her affinity is more powerful than any rational argument could support. With all its pub-crawling sordidness, it is stronger than her conventional upbringing as a minister's daughter, which deems it "more proper for it to be the man who does the loving."[9] Inequalities go much deeper than social matters; one person gives and the other receives. She is willing to go on loving a man who can from time to time give her something in return. But the intervals between those times became more difficult as they lengthened with time.

The setting of *The Deep Blue Sea,* a flat in run-down Ladbroke Grove, is as sordid as the midlands flat occupied by John Osborne's angry Jimmy

Porter. Hester Collyer and Freddie Page share a building with lower-middle-class residents of assorted identities, a common framework for Rattigan's plots. Other occupants include a failed doctor from central Europe, Mr. Miller, who practices medicine illegally when his services are needed; the landlady, Mrs. Elton, and her arthritic husband; and a young office worker and his wife, Philip and Ann Welch. The play opens with a failed suicide attempt by Hester Collyer. Rattigan begins his action where the conventional play ends and thereby dissipates the possibility for the conventional melodramatic impact of the suicide attempt. A more feeble attempt at suicide is made by Hester in Act III, and the melodrama is even further diminished, for the audience soon finds out that Rattigan has another purpose in the deployment of the suicide convention of the well-made problem play. That purpose includes a deeply poignant, Chekhovian heroine, who, like Andrew Crocker-Harris in *The Browning Version,* makes a clear, if less than confident, decision to go on living, free of the hypocrisy and the pretense that life would be without that choice.

Older than Freddie, refined in her upbringing, she chooses to leave Sir William for a mutually destructive relationship with the coarse ex-airman. She couldn't "have the comfort of killing herself. She's got to face life without him, without her husband, without her talent, without anything. She has just got to live."[10] Like Chekhov's characters, outward changes take place in her personal life, yet she remains the same, painfully aware of the changes. Life goes on even when a Cherry Orchard is sold and when Hester gives up an affluent life-style with her husband. She marks, as John Russell Taylor in his casebook on John Osborne points out, the origin of the angry young men featured in the upcoming stage revolution. Rattigan takes Hester one step further even than Osborne takes his characters in *Look Back in Anger,* for she eventually gives up Freddie Page. Osborne's unequally matched couple return to each other at the end. Bleak though it may seem, Hester's decision is the ultimate affirmation of life, beyond hope and therefore beyond despair. Rattigan moves Hester through the play to this large sense of life with sure-handed credibility. Although considered by some to be anticlimactic, the ending is, in fact, artistically and realistically right, for either of the other two resolutions—a suicide or a reconciliation with either Sir William or Freddie—would have violated the very premise of Hester's character, an unwillingness to compromise.

The finality of her condition is brought home to Hester by Miller, himself a failed and flawed character, in Rattigan's adaptation of King Lear's repetitions of the word "never" when he faced the reality of Cordelia's death:

Your Freddie has left you. He's never going to come back again.
Never in the world. Never.
At each word she wilts as if at a physical blow.
Hester. (*Wildly.*) I know. I know. That's what I can't face.
Miller. (*With brutal force.*) Yes, you can. That word "never."
    Face that and you can face life. Get beyond hope. It's your only
chance.[11]

In his preface to Volume 2 of his *Collected Plays,* Rattigan alludes to
Lear's words and also to Oswald's at the end of Ibsen's *Ghosts:* "Mother,
give me the sun." Both characters confront the finality of their losses. Lear
has lost his daughter Cordelia; with the onset of his stroke, Oswald faces
the horror of living a mindless existence. Their worlds have collapsed
around them. Similarly, Hester, after two suicide attempts, has given up
both husband and lover. Without the cosmic sweep of Lear's situation or
the hereditary-societal breadth of Oswald's, Hester's personal desperation
appears to move beyond hope to a shaky continuation of life. The sense of
tragic affirmation in Lear's regaining of his sanity and in Oswald's pleading
for the sun is there in her quiet folding of Freddie's scarf.

    The ending of the play is a brilliant *coup de théâtre* and a realistically
truthful resolution to the problem. Cameolike in its understatement, it
underscores Miller's advice, which Hester has accepted. Before Freddie
makes his final appearance to bid her good-bye and to collect his belong-
ings, she wants Miller to give her "one single reason why I should respect
myself—even a little."[12] Her request remains ungranted as the door opens
and Freddie enters. She accepts his final embrace "without in any way
returning it."[13] As the curtain falls, Hester lights the gas with a match,
turns back to the sofa, and is folding one of his scarves. Her intention to
enroll in an art school is enough to satisfy the play's emotional and artistic
requirements.

    Although conventional English attitudes toward marriage are a part of
Hester's problem, she is angry with herself rather than with society,
contributory as those social attitudes and her emotional and sexual inhibi-
tions fostered by those attitudes may be.

    Hester is a modern existentialist heroine, much larger than the usual
female victimized by current social attitudes. In speaking about her to
John Simon in 1962, Rattigan said that she was "not a sad little waif who
is suddenly carried off her feet by 'something stronger than herself,' " the
"fatal love" romanticized by the American soap-opera audience.[14]

    With her many resemblances to the women in Pinero's plays, particu-
larly Zoe of *Mid-Channel,* to whom she has been compared, she is a far cry

from the women who become victims of social strangleholds in earlier problem plays. Unlike them, she is aware of her needs and makes hard choices out of that awareness. So one does not pity her and blame society so much as feel deeply what Michael Billington calls the "inequality of most amatory relationships and a denunciation of the typically Anglo-Saxon fear of passionate emotional commitment."[15] Hester is kin to Alison in *Look Back in Anger,* who endures humiliation and pain in a marital situation similar to Hester's.

A discussion between Hester and her husband about affinities bears a curious resemblance to a recurring theme in Browning's poetry, an interesting coincidence in the light of Rattigan's earlier use of Browning's version of the *Agamemnon.* Browning's dramatic monologues and his long narratives such as *The Ring and the Book* explore the dark, irrational instincts lurking under the civilized veneers of people. And both Browning and Rattigan choose flawed, failed, and frequently desperate characters who live half-lives or whose surface lives hide deeper, buried selves.

The texture of *The Deep Blue Sea* is rich in the detail from Rattigan's own experiences that has taken on a fictional life of its own. It is a strong example of life transmuted into art: Sunningdale golfing; an ex-flyer; discussions of unjust laws that make suicide a crime; a judge; Rolls-Royces; mismatched marriages; inequality of love relationships; humiliations and loss of self-respect as tradeoffs for deeper necessities. These details and themes have been blended in near-faultless proportions.

Rattigan's own carefully guarded experiences with homosexuals, some of whom were parasitic and socially objectionable, were the basis for a double life. In both *The Deep Blue Sea* and *Separate Tables,* such experiences had to be dramatized in heterosexual form in order to get the play past the Lord Chamberlain's office. But Rattigan was always careful to emphasize that it was not so much the specific nature of the sexual relationship as it was the deeply emotional implications of that relationship with which he was concerned, so that a Hester Collyer or a Major Pollock, once shaped into a character, could not be bent back into his or her real-life origins. Critics found no fault in this play either with shifts of focus or with language. All are of a piece here. And to give a well-written play its match in performance, the first production was graced with the acting of Peggy Ashcroft, Kenneth More, and Roland Culver.

What is most surprising about the play, perhaps, is its timing. It was performed in 1952, when both Rattigan and England were enjoying a golden time, Rattigan as a successful, popular playwright and England in anticipation of a new monarch. The play partakes of none of the jubilation permeating London at that time. Instead, it exposes the underbelly of things, as the Freddie Pages and Sir William Collyers find themselves increasingly at odds with each other. Jimmy Porter seems but a step or two away from Freddie Page.

In Rattigan's gallery of heroines, Hester Collyer is a later version of Margot in *First Episode,* Diana in *French Without Tears,* Joan in *After the Dance,* Patricia in *Flare Path,* Catherine in *The Winslow Boy.* In those earlier plays, however, the heroine shares importance with other characters. In *The Deep Blue Sea,* Hester holds center stage.

In the larger gallery of modern dramatic heroines, Hester Collyer ranks with the heroines of Ibsen, Chekhov, and Tennessee Williams, for in her flawed strength she moves audiences as do Mrs. Alving, Madame Ranevskaya, and Amanda Wingfield. She also looks forward, Janus-fashion, to English heroines like Alison Porter in *Look Back in Anger* and Ruth in *The Homecoming.* These are all heroines who break with marital-code behavior in favor of emotional and sexual fulfillment.

The Sleeping Prince

But before the appearance of Alison Porter, Rattigan wrote two more plays, one a fantasy-comedy produced the next year. Subtitled "an occasional fairy tale," *The Sleeping Prince* is in the tradition of *French Without Tears, Follow My Leader, While the Sun Shines, Love in Idleness, Who Is Sylvia?*—an impressive array of comedies which variously take on qualities of farce, satire, fantasy, irony, and, now, fairy-tale romance.

The Cinderella story involves a young Carpathian king who with his regent father has arrived in London for the coronation of King George V in 1911, the year of Rattigan's birth and of coronation events in which his father took part. The play, dedicated to his mother, draws on Rattigan's familiarity with the diplomatic world of his father. The young king, like Rattigan, has strong disagreements with his father, even to the point of plotting against the regent. But in this Cinderella world father and son resolve their differences with the aid of Mary Morgan, an American actress with whom the forty-three-year-old father falls in love and who also succeeds in winning the affection of both son and mother. In a most un-Cinderella-like ending, however, the actress refuses to accompany the central European family back to Carpathia after the coronation, at least while the play in which she is currently appearing is still running on the London stage. She is independently practical in the tradition of Rattigan's heroines.

Much of the comedy, like that of *French Without Tears,* derives from Rattigan's skillful manipulation of foreign-language dialogue in German and French, as in the final offstage words spoken by the regent, an exclamation oft repeated through the play, "himmel heilige bimbaum!" These are the response to Mary's final request to him—that he send her an autographed photo of himself.

The prevailing device, however, is the oldest of all comic conventions, repetition. Each of the three members of the Carpathian royal family presents Mary with similar tokens of affection for services rendered, services which include sexual rejuvenation for the regent, companionship for the young king at the coronation ball, and attendance on the dowager at the coronation. Their tokens of affection are identical brooches, which at the end of the play she gathers up and with her two Orders of Perseverance, first and second class, puts into her handbag. "Then she firmly pulls up the collar of her mackintosh and walks out."[16]

The polished ending of a Rattigan play is nowhere more evident than in the deceptively easy naturalness with which Mary exits. In similar endings, "Millie slowly sits and begins to serve dinner" (in the *Browning Version*) and Hester (in *The Deep Blue Sea*) is quietly folding one of Freddie's scarves. Untheatrically theatrical, these endings in serious and comic dramas alike are strikingly effective in expressing the continuity and resumption of life.

Both stage and film productions of this charming tale contained as much fantasy as the play itself. For the stage version was directed by Laurence Olivier, who with his wife, Vivien Leigh, played the leading role. In the film Olivier played opposite Marilyn Monroe. It was indeed a fairy-tale opening night (retitled *The Prince and the Showgirl*) when Marilyn Monroe with her playwright-husband, Arthur Miller, along with Terence Rattigan and his mother, walked into the theater. All the tabloids featured the dazzle of the occasion. And Rattigan himself seemed caught up in the glitter of theatrical royalty present. His feelings about Olivier, especially, are contained in a piece he wrote for a book-length tribute to Olivier:

Where I had expected my flimsy little confection to be burst asunder by the vastness of his talent, it was in fact held firmly in shape by his quietly magisterial performance, which while remaining resolutely faithful to his author's frivolous intentions, succeeded in adding to the part those dimensions that one looks for from great acting; and where I had feared that my "Prince Charming" would inevitably become in his hands "Prince Utterly Irresistible," those fears were forever laid to rest when, at the dress rehearsal, I went into his dressing room just before curtain to be confronted by a rather dull-looking little man, with an anaemic complexion, a thin, prissy, humourless mouth, hair parted in the middle and plastered repulsively downwards over his ears, and a sad-looking monocle glued over his right eye. It was only when I saw that he was dressed in Edwardian evening dress, with an Order around his neck, that I recognized, and embraced, my own, true, living, breathing, Sleeping Prince. We were saved from the Tower. And I have loved the man this side of idolatry ever since—and frankly, not always "this side."[17]

For all its charm the play is second-best Rattigan but, nonetheless, a graceful complement to the two serious plays between which it appeared and a fitting conclusion to an impressive series of sunny comedies and romances.

In New York with Michael Redgrave and Barbara Bel Geddes, its reception was not as favorable as in London, owing partly to the cast change and partly to the difference between American and British humor. Still later, the play was adapted in a musical version (retitled again, *The Girl Who Came to Supper*). Even with lyrics by Noel Coward, its reception was lukewarm. All in all, for an English trifle and as an occasional piece, the play enjoyed a considerable stage run in London, as well as in its varied adaptations. The tabloids used it as a focal point for their portraiture of Rattigan as England's most successful and prosperous playwright. Certainly it dominated theatrical attention at a time when a new play by Peter Ustinov and another by N. C. Hunter appeared, the first a failure and the second a success, with Dame Sybil Thorndike, Dame Edith Evans, Irene Worth, Sir John Gielgud, and Sir Ralph Richardson.[18]

Separate Tables

It was a most auspicious time for a major play by Rattigan, and the inevitable did happen the next year (1954) with the opening of *Separate Tables*. For the third time in three successive years a play and its players were perfectly matched, with Margaret Leighton and Eric Portman in the leading roles in both plays of this twin bill. A brilliantly poignant, serious drama with subject matter akin to that of *The Deep Blue Sea*, *Separate Tables* continues Rattigan's tradition of the double bill and his practice to date of following a light drama with a serious one. And like *The Deep Blue Sea*, both of the short plays, *Table by the Window* and *Table Number Seven*, are set in a rather seedy hotel, this time in Bournemouth. The Beauregard Hotel, with its shabby gentility, resembles the residential hotel in which Rattigan's mother lived in Kensington after his father died. Rattigan visited her there frequently.

The framework of the hotel setting again allows him the freedom to assemble a variety of characters, bound mostly by their common financial plight and their plenitude of conventional English attitudes. There are two main characters in each story, whose loneliness brings them together in spite of the overwhelming incompatibilities of their natures. They stand out from the other "normal" inhabitants of the Beauregard, whom Rattigan carries over from the first to the second of the plays. In both, the eminently sensible and sensitive influence of the manageress, as a go-between between the two main characters and between each pair and the rest of the characters, is considerable. The plays, in fact, are an interesting allegory of middle-class English life in 1954, just two years before the theater was rocked by the angry and disillusioned lower-class Jimmy Porter.

Table by the Window. In the first of the two plays, Anne Shankland arrives at the Beauregard as a casual guest, as opposed to the regulars, whose residence seems indefinite. Each resident has his table in the dining room on which idiosyncratic necessities, such as pills, are kept. The characters, alone in the world except for their fellow residents, enjoy a communication of sorts in the mealtime routines and during coffee-in-the-lounge hours. Among these are Mrs. Railton-Bell and her daughter, Sibyl, who does not appear until the second play; they are obviously the most affluent of the group. The mother, by the central position of her table in the dining room, is the spokesman for the group and the dominant force in shaping group opinions on assorted matters. Mr. Fowler, a retired classics master, has fossilized into a conventional moralist. The most recent and the youngest of the guests are an unmarried couple, Charles Tanner and Jean Stratton, whose manners contrast sharply with the politeness of the other residents. They ignore each other as they eat, consumed in the reading of the moment, for Charles is a serious student of medicine. Standing apart from this group of characters are John Malcolm and Miss Cooper, he a failed journalist-politician who has retreated to Bournemouth to salvage what little he can of his writing by contributing to the *New Outlook* (evidently the fictional version of the *New Statesman*) under the pseudonym of Cato, and she the efficient and sympathetic manageress of the hotel. Their friendship is warm and close.

One senses very shortly after her arrival that Anne Shankland's intentions in choosing the Beauregard are more than just as a casual guest. Like Peter Kyle in *Flare Path,* she immediately seems out of place by her smart appearance and sophisticated manner. Suspicions are confirmed as she and John Malcolm meet, and the audience learns soon that underneath her appearance and poise is a lonely woman of forty whose two marriages have failed, the first of which was to John. A variation of Hester Collyer, she attempts desperately to pick up their relationship at the point of its breakoff. She needs him, and John, as much as ever, is irresistibly attracted to her. His more stable affection for Miss Cooper melts away in his persistently passionate response to Anne. Her need for him and his passion for her constitute affinities that characterize so many of Rattigan's characters, in spite of the destructive incompatibilities of those affinities. The force of the attraction was already dramatized in *The Deep Blue Sea,* a Strindbergian love-hate relationship that is as necessary and compelling as it is destructive.

In the course of the series of dramatic confrontations between Anne and John, we discover that he has shed his surname, Ramsden, as a protective gesture in order to hide a troublesome past. Coming from a family of eight, he states that the "gulf between Kensington Gore [London] and the Hull Docks is still fairly wide."[19] He had watched his "mother sacrifice her health, strength, and comfort and eventually her life to looking after us children, and to keeping the old man out of trouble."[20] These details are curiously interesting in the resemblance that they bear to the lower-class origins of Jimmy Porter in Osborne's play, as is the resemblance that Anne's Kensington Gore upbringing bears to that of Alison, Jimmy's wife. Social and emotional incompatibilities in both couples cause domestic strife which in the Rattigan version leads to attempted murder. The characters in Rattigan's drama are able to explain and accept each other, whereas in Osborne's play there are a series of verbal and physical explosions which lead to an exhausted acceptance of each other at the end. But in some of John's statements, he seems as savage as Jimmy:

> Because where would your fun have been in enslaving the sort of man who was already the slave of his own head gardener? You wanted bigger game. Wilder game. None of your tame baronets and Australian millionaires, too well-mannered to protest when you denied them their conjugal rights, and too well-brought-up not to take your headaches at bedtime. . . . What enjoyment would there have been for you in using your weapons on that sort of husband? But to turn them on a genuine, live, roaring savage from the slums of Hull, to make him grovel at the vague and distant promise of delights that were his anyway by right, or goad him to such a frenzy of drink and rage by a locked door that he'd kick it in and hit you with his fist so hard that you'd knock yourself unconscious against a wall—that must really have been fun.[21]

Anne counters his argument with a characterization of it as the "same old cascade of truths, half-truths and distortions, all beaten up together, to

make a neat, consistent story. *Your* story. Human nature isn't quite as
simple as you make it, John."[22] She reminds him that he has left out the
"most important fact of all,"[23] that she was fond of him. There follows a
dialogue in which the argument is equal, and they both slip into the
metaphor of marriage as a war in which his overpowering love for her, and his
"brains and the eloquence and the ability to make me [Anne] feel cheap"[24]
become weapons he uses as effectively as she has used her withholding of sex.
After the verbal release of emotions they embrace suddenly and violently,
both still realizing afterwards that for all their incompatibilities, he could
never be happy with the steady Miss Cooper nor she with anyone else but
John, tempestuous and torturous though that happiness must be. Rattigan's battle of the sexes stands alongside that dramatized by Strindberg,
Albee, Williams, and Osborne.

Anne and John's reconciliation, however, is shortlived, for in the very
next scene a telephone call to Anne from London turns out to be one from
the *New Outlook*. Humiliated by her lying and his editor's betrayal of his
whereabouts, John in a frenzy once more slips his hands on her throat and
she falls to the floor, picked up by Miss Cooper, who has just entered.

In the final scene of the play, Miss Cooper informs John that Anne's
addiction to pills is as strong as his to drink. She also reveals to him her
knowledge of his love for Anne and Anne's need of him. With forced
cheeriness, she summarizes the mismatched nature of relationships in the
play: If John had never met Anne, "she'd have been a millionairess, and
you'd have been Prime Minister and I'd have married Mr. Hopkins from
the bank, and then we'd have all been happy."[25] But things are not such.
They have all met, and it remains in the final moments of the play for John
and Anne to face a future together, both willing to risk the truth that "our
two needs for each other are like two chemicals that are harmless by
themselves, but when brought together in a test tube can make an
explosive as deadly as dynamite."[26] The play ends with the customary
Rattiganesque continuity of things as Anne, instead of departing, stays
on, and the waitress is making up a double table for her and John at lunch.

In the complexity and the openness with which that complexity is
handled, Rattigan has taken Anne and John far beyond the point he was
able to take Andrew Crocker-Harris or Hester Collyer. Their illusions and
lies are brought into the open and confronted in discussions lacking in
previous plays. Furthermore, their ability to articulate their feelings and
attitudes enjoys an equality not there in earlier characters. Unequal as the
basis for the relationship may be, need in one case and passion in the other,
both have a rational, verbalized understanding of their emotions. The

human is extended into the humanistic. Both are equal victims of themselves. Rattigan gives to Crocker-Harris some hope in his position in a new school; he leaves Hester Collyer with the vague hope of attending art school. However, Anne Shankland and John Malcolm attempt to pick up their lives where they dropped them years ago and continue, the only difference being their gained understanding of themselves, each other, and the basis for their relationship, fraught as it is with inequalities and possible exploding points. In their shaky reconciliation, they do have each other and they become, curiously, like the other residents of the Beauregard, reconciled to the human community of the hotel. John Malcolm had already made his peace with himself in his pseudonymity before Anne's arrival. His belonging is rooted in the strong friendship with Miss Cooper and in a perverse rapport with the conservative residents with whom he argues his liberal politics.

Table Number Seven. In the second of the two plays, *Table Number Seven,* the characters remain the same, except for Anne Shankland, who has been replaced by Sibyl Railton-Bell, the spinster daughter of Mrs. Railton-Bell, and John Malcolm, who gives way to Major Pollock. Another important change is that the student couple are now married and the parents of a child. Charles Stratton is still studying medicine. Most important, however, is the increased role played by the inhabitants of the hotel. In this play, they exist not only to provide background for the two major characters, but to interact with them vitally, to cause events to happen and character revelation to take place.

The main couple in *Table Number Seven* are emotionally and sexually stunted characters. Neither has the self-confidence, articulateness, or sophistication of Anne and John in the first drama. Sibyl, in her thirties, has been reared and educated solely by her mother, who has stifled any possibility for creativity or any opportunity for experience that may have been hers. Consequently, she can express her emotions only through hysterical fits, as her mother calls them. In response to Sibyl's queries about wanting to do something, her mother only reminds her of the job she held at the Jones and Jones store, which she had to leave because she was not a very strong child and because her nervous system is not nearly as sound as it should be. She is, indeed, Rattigan's version of Tennessee Williams's Laura Wingfield, unable to function or to make connections with people, privately or publicly. Of all the parent-child relationships throughout Rattigan's plays, that between Sibyl and her mother is the most damaging. At thirty-three Sibyl is still a child.

Major Pollock, in his fifties, has managed to survive with his accounts of his schooling and military experience, which turn out to be fabrications, including his title. Most important among his many fears is that of sex (as is Sibyl's), which he can express only by molesting women in dark theaters. His most recent dalliance brought arrest and newspaper publicity, and, also, the outrage of some of the residents of the Beauregard. The real-life situation from which Rattigan drew the Major's experience is homosexual, but in 1954 the Lord Chamberlain would not have approved.

The drama becomes Rattigan's first major outspoken treatment of public attitudes and their tyrannizing, brutal effect on the sensitive individual. In an earlier play, the theme took the shape of the right of the small man, Ronnie Winslow, to have his day in court. Now, however, it is not the King's Counsel whom the Major faces and fears. It is the faceless public, led by Sibyl's mother, whose talents Charles Stratton (the medical student) said could be used by Senator (Joseph) McCarthy. Rattigan was very much incensed by McCarthyism in America or England.

The conflict of the play arises from the understanding Sibyl and the Major have developed and the threat to that relationship by the newspaper account of his arrest. The actual misdemeanor or the arrest or the publicity is not as important to them as is the fear that someone, specifically Mrs. Railton-Bell, would learn of the events. They communicate with each other as only two such shy, emotionally dwarfed persons can. He admits to her that it was not the first time he had committed such offenses, and he explains to her why he has had to live by lies:

You wouldn't guess, I know, but ever since school I've always been scared to death of women. . . . I had a bad time at school—which wasn't Wellington, of course—just a council school. Boys hate other boys to be timid and shy, and they gave it to me good and proper. My father despised me, too. He was a sergeant-major in the Black Watch. He made me join the Army, but I was always a bitter disappointment to him. He died before I got my commission. I only got that by a wangle. It wasn't difficult at the beginning of the war. But it meant everything to me, all the same. Being saluted, being called sir—I thought I'm someone, now, a real person. Perhaps some woman might even—(*He stops.*) But it didn't work. It never has worked. I'm made in a certain way, and I can't change it. It has to be the dark, you see, and strangers, because—[27]

What Major Pollock left unfinished and unspoken Rattigan finishes and speaks through the schoolboys in his last play, *Cause Célèbre,* but here the damage has reached the point of incommunicability.

When Mrs. Railton-Bell, self-appointed arbiter of morals at the Beauregard, reads of the Major's arrest in the paper, she calls a meeting of the residents to vote on whether he should remain in their midst. His staunchest defender, not because he condones the action but because he believes the Major has a right to be understood, is Charles Stratton. The meeting ends on an indecisive note.

At the play's end Mr. Pollock, having shed his lies and his phony title as well, faces the icy atmosphere of the dining room where each person at his "separate table" reacts to his presence. All except Mrs. Railton-Bell offer faint, tentative recognition of him, and he is grateful for their acceptance of him into their community. In a final gesture, even the shy Sibyl for the first time in her life defies a demand from her mother that she leave the dining room. In fact, as her mother leaves, Sibyl informs the revived Mr. Pollock that there will be a new moon that night—"We must all go and look at it afterwards"—and he begins to eat his fricassee as the curtain falls. Rattigan's Chekhovian ending once more is that measured rhythm of life resumed, even by his two most psychologically crippled characters. Chekhov's metaphor of art as the moon shining on bits of broken glass applies here, as it does to the Laura Wingfields of Tennessee Williams's fictional world.

In the course of their discussions Rattigan has drawn his minor characters with the firmness, color, and credibility that has made them so favorably responded to by critics in his very first drama. For instance, there is Miss Meacham, who walks around with her nose in the racing pages of the paper and seems oblivious to everything and everyone else. And although in her expected straightforward manner she says she does not give a damn about a dirty old man, she does in her own way show an offhand, but real, concern for him at the end by speaking to the Major, defying the authority of Mrs. Railton-Bell in doing so. Delightfully idiosyncratic, she states that she does not want her nieces visiting her as in her they would only see themselves in the future. Rattigan humorously inverts conventional attitudes of older people who enjoy having the young around, either to remind them of their youth or to feel young once more. Miss Meacham, flaunting convention, constructs her own rules for life and, consequently, can break them with impunity and without injury to others. With each scene she and the other Beauregard residents take on an importance they do not have in *Table by the Window*.

But it is Miss Cooper who functions as Rattigan's raisonneur in the drama. As one who has loved someone once and will always continue to do so, she confides to Mr. Pollock, she can be cheerful "because there's no point in being anything else. I've settled for the situation, you see, and it's surprising how cheerful one can be when one gives up hope. I've still got the memory, you see, which is a very pleasant one—all things considered."[28] In her quiet manner she makes him feel welcome to stay on at the hotel, even before she says so. Once more, a failed character, painfully aware of his flaws, has been redeemed by his own courage and by having gained the sympathy of the conventionally attuned community whose acceptance he so desperately needs.

In *Separate Tables* Rattigan has finely spun the stories of four lonely people damaged by life, lost, and then redeemed by the same forces. Repressive hypocrisy of sexual attitudes and emotional expression nowhere in his other work produce the emotional tension and its release as in this drama. Although society's intolerance of aberrational behavior is not wiped out, it is diminished by the common sense of humanity, the bond that above every other is Rattigan's "bottom line."

Illuminated by the superb acting of Margaret Leighton and Eric Portman, the psychological honesty of the characters rang true for audiences and critics. Play and players were acclaimed in England and America, and Miss Leighton won the Tony award in New York for her performance.

For this writer, *Separate Tables* remains Rattigan's major drama. Anne Shankland and John Malcolm have a place in the long line of modern dramatic antagonists begun by Strindberg in plays such as *Dance of Death, The Father,* and *Miss Julie,* in which the battle of the sexes rages full scale. Continued in Tennessee Williams's *A Streetcar Named Desire* and Edward Albee's *Who's Afraid of Virginia Woolf?,* the struggle for sexual and psychological supremacy develops into a battle for survival. Until *Separate Tables,* no British dramatist of the twentieth century had dealt so passionately with the battle of the sexes.

Similarly, Sibyl and the Major belong to a more delicate tradition of modern characters whose fate has been determined early in life by circumstances beyond their control and who have, consequently, little strength or ability to cope with life. For them there are only the evasions and the illusions with which to nourish hope. Like Hedvig of Ibsen's *The Wild Duck* and Laura of Williams's *The Glass Menagerie,* Sibyl, much older than either Hedvig or Laura, can live only in a hothouse. In real life all three cannot even survive without the supports of the very type of existence which caused their emotional damage in the first place. Hedwig shoots herself. Laura Wingfield, with her clubfoot and overly protective but well-meaning mother, can only become sick in typing school. Sibyl becomes sick in the basement of the Jones and Jones department store during her one brief and abortive foray into the outside world. None of the women possess even the ability of Major Pollock to manage the externalities of life. In spite of painful exposures occasionally, he has at least managed to survive, even if only by lies.

Both Sibyl and Major Pollock move an audience by the sheer, exquisite frailty of their sensitivity to each other. They awaken in the other characters a sensitiveness, forgotten or deeply buried in conventional attitudes, with their plea for social tolerance. In the prevailing dramatic tradition of social alienation, Rattigan's reconciliation of society with the individual is a refreshing affirmation of life. Scorned by angry or absurdist characters in many modern plays, social acceptance or at least social tolerance is desperately needed by John Malcolm, Sibyl Railton-Bell, and Major Pollock. The interdependence of the individual and his society, strong in Rattigan's early plays, still exerts its pull on the characters. Since the common bond among the residents of the Beauregard is the separateness of each person, all four leading characters qualify for membership in the community. As a group the residents function as antagonist to the protagonists, Sibyl and the Major. Between the two groups Rattigan manages a reconciliation of sorts, mostly because each of the residents, having already made his own peace with the world, can extend the same opportunity to the newcomers.

Each scene moves unswervingly in this direction. And even the first play, a complete drama in itself, moves toward the characterizations and actions of the second, serving as partial exposition of the latter. In no other play of Rattigan's does the diversity within unity emerge so satisfyingly in the artistic whole of the play. The separateness and loneliness of each person are the basis for both diversity and unity. Even Charles and Jean Stratton, single in the first play, married and parents in the second, are well on the road to their separateness as Jean is developing with their child the same type of relationship by which Mrs. Railton-Bell caused the emotional dwarfing of Sibyl.

Rattigan's favorite framework device—the grand hotel—is effectively used in his depiction of states of loneliness among a variety of social outcasts, each of whom has learned in his way to deal with that loneliness and its pain. The framework affords opportunity for rich contrasts of various segments of middle-class English society who are integrated in a realistic and dramatically satisfying whole. Gorki chose such a structure for his *The Lower Depths,* Eugene O'Neill for *The Iceman Cometh,* and Tennessee Williams for *Small Craft Warnings.* Rattigan's *Separate Tables* takes no second place in this impressive tradition. Having used the framework in earlier plays, he has perfected the structural technique in *Separate Tables*, which won so many honors for him.

Even though the taboos of the time kept Rattigan from dramatizing the Major as a homosexual, he did have his characters talk freely to each other, Anne to John, and Major Pollock to Sibyl, about their sexual needs in language that for England in 1954 was free. The Major shyly suggests to Sibyl that she is "so scared of—well—shall we call it life? It sounds more respectable than the word which I know you hate. You and I are awfully alike, you know. That's why I suppose we've drifted so much together in this place."[29] He is, of course, painting Sibyl with his own fear of normal sexual experience. Later to Miss Cooper, Sibyl repeats the conversation, taking it one step further as she actually uses the word "sex." "He says we're both scared of life and people and sex. There—I've said the word. He says I hate *saying* it even, and he's right. I do."[30] The Major's frank confession of his sexual aberrations and the reason for them and Sibyl's free expression of her feared abnormality are Rattigan's frankest criticism up to this time of sexual taboos. The damage caused by society in the persons of Mrs. Railton-Bell and the Major's father is far greater than that caused by the resulting abnormal sexual behavior of their victims. The verbal frankness of Sibyl and the Major is necessary not only to reach their mutual understanding but as a corrective measure for repressive social attitudes. In both characters the verbalization of their conditions frees them to act, reminiscent of the experience of Crocker-Harris in *The Browning Version.*

Of all the flawed and failed protagonists in Rattigan's plays, Sibyl and the Major are the most delicately poignant, and their halting, limited, yet painfully free confessions reflect Rattigan's effortlessness with naturalistic speech patterns which underlie the authentic characterizations and the seamlessness of the scenes.

There was unanimous critical and popular acclaim of *Separate Tables* as enlightened theater. Describing Margaret Leighton's and Eric Portman's brilliant and moving performances as "economy of means," Brooks Atkinson wrote that it is the same economy of means with which Rattigan wrote the play, so that it would be impossible to distinguish one from the other.[31]

Chapter Eleven
Morality Plays for Mid-Century or Man, God, and the Devil

A New Hero: Jimmy Porter

During the long two-year West End run of *Separate Tables,* the inevitable occurred. The long-awaited stage revolution finally erupted on 8 May 1956. Its force unleashed repressions of the economic-cultural anger in post–World War II England and disrupted prevailing stage conventions. Writers, actors, directors—indeed the entire theatrical community—felt the impact of the history-making *Look Back in Anger* by John Osborne. Its leading character is the angry young Jimmy Porter, trapped in a dead-end existence in the midlands of England and also trapped in his marriage. For him there are no more great causes, and so he turns his frustrations and anger on his wife, genteel Alison Porter, and on their long-suffering friend, Cliff Lewis, with whom Jimmy operates a sweets stall. The people he loves most are the only means by which he can exorcise his anger. In a world of no exits, he makes them his only exit. In spite of the cruel treatment he receives, Cliff serves as a buffer between the volatile Jimmy and the passive Alison. In doing so, he becomes with Alison the object of Jimmy's frustrated passions. Bitter in his verbal and physical expression of anger, Jimmy vents his feelings on whoever and whatever are in his path. Even as one emotional upheaval subsides another is already forming, allowing its victim little or no time to recover from the previous one. Alison reels from Jimmy's love-hate actions until she can bear no more. Discovering she is pregnant, she leaves him without revealing her pregnancy. Meantime, Helena, an old actress-friend of Alison's, moves in and assumes Alison's place. At the conclusion of the play she leaves and Alison returns, having lost her child. Both she and Jimmy are exhausted from their journeys back to families and friends who love them, and they resume their life with all the illusions gone and the emotion having taken its toll on them. Both accept the truth of their cultural and psychological incompatibilities, yet realize their obsessive need for each other and that each is all the other has. They seem very close indeed to the characters of Hester Collyer and Freddie Page, Anne Shankland and John Malcolm, and other variations of these characters in Rattigan's dramas.

Yet it is Jimmy Porter who has become the legendary antihero of modern British drama. The generation of the 1930s, highly idealistic, channeled its idealism into the Spanish Civil War. The succeeding generation found similar outlet and purpose in World War II, a struggle that developed into one of sheer survival for England. In the 1950s, however, no such outlet existed for the lower-class, university-educated, intelligent, sensitive person. Jimmy can look forward to nothing beyond the running of a sweets stall in a midlands town and living in an oppressively dreary flat, *ménage à trois* fashion, where frustrated emotions constantly rise to the boiling point. Values seem not to exist, or they exist in a vacuum. They tend, such as they are, to be highly personal, having no connection with the existing societal structure and social consciousness. Consequently, there is not even anything to rebel against except one's self and those most intimately related. The Strindbergian torture which Jimmy imposes on Alison is his self-flagellation. For him and for her as well, the concluding reconciliation is one of exhaustion, their futures seeming not less bleak than at the beginning of the play.

Ironically, the structure and style of Osborne's play are at best conventional, and it remained for Harold Pinter, at the same time as the emergence of Osborne's antihero, to introduce the first real and certainly influential experimentation in these respects. Osborne's surfaces and dramatic narrative are naturalistic, as are Ibsen's and Strindberg's and Rattigan's. In conventional modern dramatic fashion, he takes his characters into their pasts, where the roots of the present are to be found. Like Norah of Ibsen's *A Doll's House*, Alison is partly revealed by her association with an animal—a squirrel, Jimmy by a bear. The secret on which the plot turns, so important to the Scribean well-made play, is Alison's pregnancy, withheld from Jimmy until late in the action. The domestic triangle of Jimmy, Alison, and Cliff (later Helena) is a 1956 version of similar marital problems in Ibsen's or Strindberg's or Rattigan's plays. The teeter-totter action of the psychological, sometimes physical, struggle contains the tensions of the well-made problem play, including the big scene, the *scène à faire*.

Traditional though its structure and style are, its importance lies in the no-holds-barred honesty, the sheer brutal force, and the animal magnetism that characterize the marriage of Jimmy and Alison. For the first time on the modern English stage uninhibited expression of complex passions, contradictory and violent feelings totally unleashed, with their paradoxical mixture of irrational impulses and reasoned attitudes, created a succession of emotional scenes which left the audience as drained as are the characters in the play.

The year of the play was 1956, and its stage home was the experimental Royal Court Theatre in Sloane Square, which became the residence not only for Osborne's plays but for other new writers whose plays could be given opportunities of production. In addition to providing such opportunities, the Royal Court enjoys historical importance in its launching of the stage revolution which was to stigmatize earlier playwrights and their work as "old-fashioned," "French-window," "well-made." Rattigan felt keenly the stigma of the label and never quite recovered from the injury.

In fact, he attended the opening of *Look Back in Anger,* after which he made his well-known, oft-repeated comment about the impact of Osborne's play. He said that the future basis for reaction to plays would be, "Look how unlike Rattigan I'm being."[1] For a few critics such as Kenneth Tynan, Rattigan became the whipping boy as the embodiment of the old-fashioned play.

Yet Rattigan was not the old-fashioned playwright or the slick dramatist of public-school virtue and traditional English values, as his critics frequently accused him. For all his light-hearted comedies such as *French Without Tears* and for all his concern with upper-middle-class characters, one can go as far back as his first play, *First Episode,* to begin tracing the disillusionment that would find such brutally honest expression in the lower-middle-class characters of Osborne in 1956. The disenchantment of Jimmy Porter hangs heavily in the post–World War I and pre–World War II generations in *After the Dance.* The common cause of World War II temporarily dissipated the emotional dissatisfactions and marital mismatches, although these were present in his war drama, *Flare Path.* Once more they became the subject of his dramas after the war and continued to become increasingly important with every play, reaching their highest intensity in the flawed and failed characters of Andrew Crocker-Harris, Hester Collyer, Anne Shankland and John Malcolm, Sibyl Railton-Bell and Major Pollock, Lydia and Sebastian Crutwell, and in the historical characters of Alexander, Ross, and Nelson.

The tension of Rattigan's plays essentially consists of the ambivalence created by the gap between deep-seated, complex emotional needs of the characters and their upper-middle-class sensibilities and composure which restrained them from satisfying or expressing those needs.

Consequently, the ambivalence created pain, failure, and social ostracism which forced them to find whatever means necessary to survive. However, unlike the fate of the alienated characters of the new drama, Rattigan's emphasis in resolving the problems of his characters was reintegration into the human community by means of their choice of a life in some segment of their society. Individuality and community are equally necessary forces in their lives. Isolation and alienation function only as a means toward the end of community, not as an end in themselves. The Hester Collyers and Alma Rattenburys are a means of integrating the Aunt Ednas and the Mrs. Davenports with social pariahs by the painfully slow process of increased tolerance of unconventional behavior and attitudes and by increased awareness of the emotional injury caused by ignorance, particularly in sexual and marital matters.

Curiously enough, Rattigan did not rely on the more obvious techniques of the Scribean well-made play, such as withheld secrets, to complicate his plots and create tension, frequently false and at best mechanical. What secrets may exist are openly handled and disclosed in plays such as *The Winslow Boy, The Browning Version, The Deep Blue Sea, Separate Tables,* etc. They certainly do not constitute the big scene or the climactic moment even in the comedies.

Osborne's *Look Back in Anger,* on the other hand, makes obvious use of the devices. In fact, both Osborne and Joe Orton have been described as old-fashioned in structure and techniques, shockingly frank as their subject matter and language were at the time. The importance of their work was recognized by Rattigan, much as he felt injured by the peremptory critical dismissal of his own. He invested financially in Joe Orton's plays; he admired Pinter's work and was a friend of the Pinter family; he admired Osborne's work, frequently calling attention to the well-made-play style of this former actor, who epitomized all that seemed to be new, even as Rattigan became the embodiment of the old.

Finally, differences between the English stage before and after 1956 seem to consist of two major changes. One of these changes is the admission onto the stage of characters from the lower classes as worthy of serious attention, rather than as secondary, frequently comic, figures or as victims of society to be pitied. The second is the total freedom to use whatever language and experience is appropriate to the expression of that character. After repeal of censorship laws in the late 1960s, distinction between the kind of play put on by theaters such as the Royal Court and that staged by West End theaters diminished.

The new freedoms of the English stage became obvious in Rattigan's remaining plays. In particular, the next three plays illustrate a remarkable shift in subject matter that was obliquely and discreetly handled, sometimes disguised, in his earlier work. Although basic themes have not changed, their increasing complexity and closeness to real-life situations from which they are derived are more frankly sexual. He said that he wanted to "blow up the establishment" by writing a confessional play about homosexuality. At the time, a report (Wolfendon) was being prepared to begin repeal of the law which made homosexuality a crime. In fact, the report is alluded to in *Variation on a Theme*. His next three plays, wedged between the 1956 debut of Jimmy Porter and Rattigan's 1963 self-exile from the England stage, are open in their treatments of homosexual characters: *Variation on a Theme, Ross,* and *Man and Boy*.

Variation on a Theme

Variation on a Theme (1958) appeared four years after *Separate Tables,* a significant fact in the light of the close succession of his plays during the 1940s and early 1950s. Certainly work on film versions of *Who Is Sylvia?, The Deep Blue Sea,* and *The Sleeping Prince* (as well as an unproduced script for *Lawrence of Arabia*) occupied much of his time. And although readjustments in personal affairs made claims on his time, it was the new turn of English stage history that had something to do with the four-year hiatus in his stage writing.

Whatever the reasons for the prolonged absence of a new play, *Variation on a Theme,* dedicated, "with deep gratitude and affection, to Margaret Leighton for whom this play was most eagerly written and by whom it was most brilliantly played" (direction by John Gielgud), opened on 8 May 1958, during a time when Osborne and Pinter were commanding the lion's share of critical attention. Even with Margaret Leighton in the leading role, however, its run, as Rattigan runs go, was a short one, contrasting with the 513 performances of *The Deep Blue Sea* and the 726 of *Separate Tables.*

Set in a villa in Cannes, France, it is the story of Rose Fish, married four times to rich husbands and on the verge of still another marriage. This time the prospective husband is a German tycoon by the name of Kurt

Mast, who has acquired his wealth on the black market of World War II. Their impending marriage, however, is thwarted as a result of Rose's meeting with a ballet dancer, Anton Valov, who turns out to be Ron Vale, from the same general Birmingham origins as Rose. After dropping the assumed name and accent at the beginning of the play, he develops a relationship with Rose because he needs her money and love and she needs to give both. At the time of their meeting, Ron is involved in a homosexual relationship with Sam Duveen, director-choreographer.

In his characterization of Ron, Rattigan develops the theme of the strong influence of the younger on the older person as the main idea of the play. Ron is twenty-six and Rose is in her mid-thirties. Inequalities are compounded by Fiona, Rose's teen-age daughter by her first husband and an aspiring actress who refuses to allow Rose to love her. Only Hettie, an impoverished noblewoman who serves as Rose's loyal, paid companion, seems to reciprocate genuine love. Inequality of love relationships, particularly those in which the recipient is less than worthy of love, is richly developed in the drama. Rattigan's is, indeed, a realistic version of the nineteenth-century Camille story.

The narrative lacks the tautness of *Separate Tables* and is more closely allied to the looser, Chekhovian "states of being" drama in which people talk and talk. After a series of duologues in which Rose discusses her emotional needs frankly and honestly and we discover the emotional states of the other characters, Rose finally decides to leave Kurt, knowing that her living with Ron does not contain even the element of a gamble. For she knows that her ignoring the doctor's advice to move to Switzerland—she has consumption—means her imminent death. In unmelodramatic fashion she states that she's "always imagined an end far more lurid and horrifying than a winter in Cannes with a man I love more than life. More than life? Silly phrase, that—isn't it? Just a woman's exaggeration."[2] Her self-parody is Rattigan's way of deflating an emotionally poignant moment to avoid the possibility of mawkish sentimentality. The melodrama of this "Camille" is tempered by Rose's realistic assessment of her state and by the choice made in a responsible awareness of the consequences.

Perhaps the most revealing dialogue in the play is that between Rose and Sam as they talk about Ron, who has just left Sam for Rose. Confessing her need for loving someone even when that love cannot be returned, Rose hears Sam's explanation of Ron:

You don't seem to understand that the Rons of this world always end by hating the people they need. They can't help it. It's compulsive. Of course it probably isn't plain hate. It's love–hate, or hate–love, or some other Freudian jargon—but it's still a pretty good imitation of the real thing. You see—when day after day, night after night—you're being kicked hard and steadily in the teeth, it's not all that important what the character who's doing it feels for you. You can leave that to the psychiatrist to work out. All you can do is to nurse a broken jaw and, in your own good time, get the hell out. I'll give you six months—from the honeymoon. Take a bet?[3]

Without passion, Sam then describes Ron's staging a phony suicide scene because of his strong jealousy of another young ballet dancer. In response to Sam's characterization of Ron's professional mediocrity and his personal liaisons, Rose explains why she has decided to stay with Ron. "It's just because his needing me is—well—the best thing that's ever happened to me, and without it I wouldn't see much point in going on living. That's not a woman's exaggeration, Sam. It's the simple truth. I can't explain why it means so much. Hettie quoted Horace at my head the other day. Something about expelling Nature with a pitchfork, but it always comes back. Meaning, I suppose, that since Birmingham I've suppressed my natural instincts, and now Nature has taken a mean revenge—"[4]

Sam brutally accuses Rose of turning the tables on Nature "by taking a boy nine years younger than you and turning him from a fairly good virtuoso dancer into a male Rose Fish."[5] With conversations such as these constituting much of the play's content, Rattigan conducts an ongoing debate between nurture and nature without the lean, spare dialogue of earlier plays that leaves much of the meaning to the implicit or unspoken. Here the explicit dominates, and much of the emotional tension is dissipated. Reference to "a male Rose Fish" is a naked statement that makes awkward its disguise of a homosexual character. In *Separate Tables* the disguise became so natural that it could not be bent back. The very calm, rational debate—in fact, a long discussion—about Ron by Rose and Sam as a substitute for the dramatic tension in the less verbalized earlier plays results in something like self-parody on the part of the author.

Yet the *scène à faire* of the play, a card game between Ron and Kurt, does restore, although with theatricality, some of the lost tension. The game subtly develops into a classical morality duel in which each fights his battle for Rose. When he wins, Ron flings the money at Rose to express his rejection of his parasitic dependence on her money. However, she prevents a fist fight between the two men by coming between them. Very deftly Rattigan builds up to this "big scene" and just as deftly deflates it of the conventional theatricality.

But the real conflict occurs within each of the two main characters, Rose and Ron. Their decisions are not made blindly, for she is aware of her impending death and he of his potentially mediocre ballet career. Their emotional inequality is dramatized with brilliance rather than in the poignantly moving manner of *Separate Tables.* Rattigan's laying out all his dramatic "cards on the table" did not "blow up the establishment," but his free working in a less disguised fashion was, indeed, a variation on a theme that carries its own impact.

The obsessive need to love, even when that love is unreturned or its object unworthy, and the need to express that love, are etched with sharper and more explicit naturalistic surfaces than in the earlier dramas and make the narrative a fascinating variation on earlier characters who could not articulate their needs and frustrations. The pain and humiliation, preferable at all costs to the repressions of the Camille-like love of Rose and Ron, are the result of rational choices made by both with existentially clear awareness of the consequences.

On another level, the psychological and autobiographical subject matter is intimately Rattigan's. "Chips" Channon, an American who had married into the British upper class, enjoyed a close relationship with Rattigan similar to that of Kurt and Rose. Early liaisons with older men and later ones with younger men are variously treated in the characters of Rose, Ron, Sam, and Kurt. But if the play draws on personal experiences, the truths of those experiences have freed themselves of the factual realities in which they originate.

In addition, Rattigan wrote the play for Margaret Leighton, who had become a close friend. Even though her unhappy marriage to Laurence Harvey was in part another source for the drama, it would be difficult to draw close parallels, as the fictional truths create their own characters and situations.

The cultural mileu of the times, especially the literary scene, receives its share of attention in the play in the person of Rose's young daughter, Fiona. For her, existentialism, the angry young men, and James Deanery are old-fashioned. She has a novelist friend who writes about "a lot of young people who have love affairs with each other and don't much enjoy it, but go on doing it because there isn't any point in doing anything else."[6] Her attitude resembles the mood of the 1939 characters of *After the Dance,* the 1948 views on art in *Harlequinade,* and, in their fullest form, the state of the arts in their times by the characters in *In Praise of Love* in 1973. The views are expressed frequently as a conflict between fathers and sons or between old and new generations. There are few plays of Rattigan's in which a youthful character does not serve importantly in this capacity. *Variation on a Theme* finds kinship with the type of drama Tennessee Williams wrote about rich, older American women in relationships with young men in Italy who needed above everything else to give love and/or sex by whatever means necessary. Rattigan's Rose is not so bizarre, certainly, but neither does she emerge in as sympathetic a role as his earlier heroines, and this fact may account in part for the mixed critical reception. In fact, Shelagh Delaney, incensed by Rattigan's treatment of a homosexual relationship, particularly with Margaret Leighton in the leading role, wrote *A Taste of Honey* to express her views of the subject in what she felt was a much more sensitive treatment.

Ross

If *Variation on a Theme* enjoyed neither the critical nor popular success of Rattigan's other plays of that decade, it was more than compensated for in his next play, *Ross* (1960), with whose performance he began his fourth decade of writing for the stage. Not since *French Without Tears* in 1936 and *While the Sun Shines* in 1942, with their respective 1,030 and 1,154 runs, had a London production of his enjoyed such success.

What made its success stand out was that in that same London season Harold Pinter's *The Caretaker* and Arnold Wesker's *Roots* opened, and the English stage was luxuriating in Shakespearean productions at the Old Vic and the Aldwych. *Ross* more than held its own among the dramatic excitements of that year.

When it opened in New York with John Mills (in London Alec Guinness played the lead), its reception was equally strong. "Gripping Hit" (*Journal American*),[7] "John Mills Triumphs" (*Daily News*),[8] "'Ross' Magnificent Study of a Legend" (*New York Mirror*)[9] read the tabloid headlines. In the *New York Times* Howard Taubman began his review by ranking it with Tennessee Williams's *The Night of the Iguana* as "two notable plays" that "pay the theatre the compliment of regarding it as a place where the sources of man's nature may be explored with boldness and wonder. They adorn the theatre by bringing to it disciplined craftsmanship, distinction of style and integrity of purpose. With these plays the tone of the Broadway season gains greatly in quality."[10] In New York as well as in London *Ross* rivaled the best theater offerings of the season.

Recipient of such accolades, *Ross* was an auspicious revival of Rattigan from the blow dealt him by the New Wave critics and particularly from the mixed notices of *Variation on a Theme*.

Once more at the beginning of a new decade Rattigan returned to an historical theme. A dramatic portrait of the legendary T. E. Lawrence, *Ross* reflects Rattigan's lifelong interest in historical characters, beginning with the schoolboy play about Cesar Borgia and his reading of history at Oxford. Like the leading character in *After the Dance* (1939), who is a writer of history, Rattigan at times felt that he, too, should have chosen that career. His history plays are an artful wedding of two important interests.

Like *Adventure Story, Ross* is on its most obvious level concerned with the rise and fall of an historical hero whose actions in the drama turn on the question of identity. In the earlier play Alexander asks, "Where did I go wrong?" Now Lawrence of Arabia, who believes firmly at the outset in the Greek injunction to "Know Thyself," asks himself, "Oh Ross—how did I become you?" The episodic narrative of both historical plays leads to a question asked by each of the two heroes.

Lawrence knows that his strength lies in the strong will by which he controls and therefore directs himself and others. He exercises his will quietly in his influence over his Arab friends and very actively in the battles in which he engages the Turks. In the climactic moment of his life, Lawrence's will is broken by Turkish captors who violate him sexually, thereby destroying the will by which he was able to repress his own homosexuality, or to sublimate it in the Arabian dream. Having such a specific focus for his portrait of Lawrence, Rattigan was able to tighten the episodic narrative with eight very brief and equally taut scenes in each of the two acts by creating a tension lacking in *Variation on a Theme* and lacking also in *Adventure Story*. The concentration is so masterful that the play seems seamless even with its episodic style.

The framework for the narration of Lawrence's Arabian adventure is his enlistment in the Royal Air Force at Uxbridge under the assumed name of Ross. He hopes his new identity will provide him with the anonymity he has chosen as his means of survival. However, a fellow serviceman discovers his secret and reveals it to the newspapers, resulting in Ross's departure from the base at the end of the play, to continue his search for anonymity in still another identity as Shaw. Between arrival at and departure from Uxbridge there is the dream-reenactment of the English-Arab conflict with the Turks, in which Lawrence played a powerful and enigmatic role.

The Uxbridge framework for the Arabian episodes provided Rattigan with an effective structure from real life. Like the provincial hotel in *Flare Path* and the Beauregard in *Separate Tables,* Uxbridge allowed past events as they gathered retrospective momentum to merge subtly into Ross's move into still another attempt at anonymity.

Lawrence's mystical political faith in the Arabs' right to govern themselves is the motivation for his rise from cartographer for the British military to Arab confidante who inspired in superiors and aides alike the fierce loyalty that is the special brand of Arabs. He worked with a quietness and unassuming force which his British and Turkish superiors or equals tended to see as arrogance but which the common run of military personnel and "the uncommon" superiors such as General Allenby and Auda Abu Tayi sensed to be a profound clarity, wisdom, and honesty.

The three parallel scenes, in which Lawrence earns the respect of Auda, Allenby and, with disastrously negative consequences, the Turkish general, illustrate Rattigan's mastery of scene construction, in which leanness and implicitness of dialogue are at their best.

In the first of the three, the theatrical irony is brilliant. After discussing the military realities of the Arabs, a Turkish captain arrives to negotiate with Auda, in the presence of Lawrence, the capture of this fanatic Englishman. His offer is a set of false teeth for Auda, just as in the opening scenes there is a price to be extracted by Dickinson from either the newspaper or Lawrence himself for the revelation or concealment of Ross's identity. Auda carries his joke so far as to ask Lawrence, dressed as an Arab, to escort the captain out of the tent. Both men laugh about the joke they have just played on the Turk, even as Auda looks longingly at the fragments his rifle has just made of the false teeth.

In a second equally forceful scene with General Allenby, Lawrence's ability to inspire respect is further dramatized. Allenby's fear of the intellectual superiority of Lawrence is quickly dismissed when the latter incorrectly identifies the date of an alabaster perfume jar which he had presented to the general. Lawrence smilingly receives Allenby's correction, and the tension breaks. The two find they have reading interests in common; in addition Lawrence had made it a point to learn of Allenby's interests in "Shakespeare, Chippendale, mobile warfare, Chopin and children."[11] The tension of a first meeting relieved, both men proceed to discuss military strategy and, even more importantly, matters of self-knowledge, belief, and the ability to will one's self into a belief. The last point, in the form of a question to Lawrence, is significant as it is Lawrence's will that the Turks later break by their homosexual rape of him.

With the breaking of that will came the loss of belief in his dream and the subsequent searches for peace under assumed identities of Ross and Shaw. The third parallel occurs two scenes later. The audience is prepared for it by a short conversation between the Turkish general and captain in which the former discussed Lawrence as a man with two faiths: one in the Arabs' readiness for statehood, and the other, "more vulnerable—what I hear he calls his bodily integrity."[12] Like Allenby they have done their homework well. But unable to get Lawrence to recant his first faith, they proceed by rape to destroy the second. After the sexual violation, the general explains to Lawrence the reason:

I do pity you, you know. You won't ever believe it, but it's true. I know what was revealed to you tonight, and I know what that revelation will have done to you. You can think I mean just a broken will, if you like. That might have destroyed you by itself. But I mean more than that. Far more. (*Angrily.*) But why did you leave yourself so vulnerable? What's the use of learning if it doesn't teach you to know yourself as you really are?. . . For you, killing wasn't enough.[13]

The Turkish general's intelligence of Lawrence had gone beyond that of Auda and Allenby, and the Turk's violence on Lawrence ironically carried out the early conversations between Allenby and Lawrence on the matter of will. Even to Allenby and Auda, Lawrence's unwillingness to be touched and his talent for self-concealment were known, so that his rape by the Turks is subtly and credibly prepared for. Lawrence's flaw is self-concealment, and the Greek *hubris* (a word used in the play) is very much the theme of Rattigan's psychological portrait of Lawrence.

Lawrence's assumed identities were the means by which he sought the peace he talks about to his Uxbridge acquaintances. In the final scene of the play, the sympathetic efforts of his comrades to keep him in their company is a first step in that direction. When Parsons indignantly comments on the way Ross is being treated as the "most dirtiest, bleedingest trick that even those bastards have ever pulled on one of us," Lawrence quietly questions, "On one of us?"[14] His earlier belief in himself and in the Arabian dream destroyed, he welcomes the simply human sympathy of the sergeant, who expresses the men's intentions to help Ross, because there's no one "in this world who can't be made to fit in somehow—"[15] Both separateness and community are necessary for his survival. In the tradition of Rattigan's endings, Ross "looks round the hut for the last time and then shouldering his kitbag, he follows the Flight Sergeant out."[16] Again there is the Chekhovian continuity of life. Ross's search for peace will continue under still another identity. The peace he searches for is community on an anonymous basis that would allow him a measure of separateness within that community.

Those early attempts of Rattigan in *French Without Tears* to construct scenes in a Chekhovian manner have matured into the lean tautness of the episodes in *Ross* in which implicit truths about the characters are effectively drawn.

Most reviews of the play referred to the fact that Rattigan had completed a film script for *Lawrence of Arabia,* whose shooting was postponed and eventually canceled. Later a screen version by Robert Bolt was filmed, but Michael Darlow regards Rattigan's script as being superior to Bolt's. In any event, the screenplay was partly responsible for the dramatic polish to *Ross* which his other history plays may have lacked.

Like the plays it preceded and followed, *Ross* is a play about a homosexual subject, handled without the need for disguises or apology or even the need to shock the establishment. The specific sexual problem could just as easily have been of another sort, and its truths would have remained intact. Dealt with as an intensely human condition, without affectation, stereotypes, or propagandistic intent to increase public tolerance, the subject matter takes on natural rhythms of historical event and private experience. In *Ross* implicitness, focus, and seamless flow of dramatic narrative are at their best.

Finally, *Ross* is Rattigan's last successful stageplay before, under the impact of personal events and professional disappointment, he turned from the stage to films. The very question which Lawrence asks himself at the end of Act I, "Oh Ross—how did I become you?", is the question that Rattigan frequently asked himself from 1960 until 1970, when once more he returned to the London stage with *A Bequest to the Nation.*

Man and Boy

In the immediate post-1956 period, Rattigan wrote a third but less successful play, *Man and Boy,* in which homosexuality was openly handled, although not of primary interest in the narrative. This time one of the major confidence men of the twentieth century, Ivar Kreuger, is fictionalized in his relationship to a son who had disowned him and is now living in a small Greenwich Village, New York, apartment.

The thickly plotted play involves Gregor Antonescu, who uses his illegitimate son's apartment in the Village to extricate himself from the most catastrophic financial situation of his career. Having been involved in

the shady financial schemes of his father, the disillusioned son had broken
with him five years earlier and has seen nothing of him since. A struggling
pianist, he lives in a cheap Greenwich Village apartment with an actress,
Carol Penn. He knows nothing of his father's present scheme until
suddenly Gregor shows up, revealing nothing of his real purpose but
asking the use of the apartment. A parasitic aide, Sven, has now replaced
Basil in his father's manipulations.

The current confidence game entails the softening of a public announcement of the failure of an Antonescu merger with the holdings of
American Electric, whose executive head, Herries, is a homosexual. The
weapons Gregor employs to achieve the softening are his knowledge of
Herries's homosexual affair with Harter and the use of Basil Antonescu as
homosexual bait for Herries. Both prove abortive when the newspaper
headlines scream the news that the FBI, having been informed of forged
collaterals in a recent Bank of London scandal, is looking for Antonescu.
Basil, who had furiously left the apartment upon realizing what his father
was up to, returns with the newspapers to inform Gregor and Sven. One by
one wife and colleagues desert Gregor, who even helps Sven plan his own
suicide. Only Basil refuses to leave him. As it began, the play ends with
the radio blaring the latest news about the swindler.

On one level the play deals with the struggle within Antonescu to live
without a conscience. Up to this time he has managed so successfully he
did not need the love that boy could offer man. Now it is all he has left, and
with the vanishing of his world, he acknowledges that the roles of man and
boy are reversing. "Who is now the strong and who the weak?"[17] Beyond
disillusion himself, Gregor attempts to disillusion Basil by branding as
sentimental lies the stories about his (Gregor's) boyhood. His attempt to
discard the very idea of a conscience is rejected by Basil, and at one moving
point they embrace in a scene reminiscent of the Willy Loman–Biff
relationship in Arthur Miller's *Death of a Salesman*. It is the only emotion
that Gregor has allowed himself in a long time, very much like the
emotional release of Andrew Crocker-Harris in *The Browning Version*. It is
indeed a refutation of Gregor's own contention that he has no conscience
and an affirmation of the Rattiganesque need for belonging to humanity.
Yet even this brief emotional moment cancels itself out in Gregor's last
words to his son: "Whatever happens never, in the future, let the truth
make you cry."[18] Basil's response is "I won't—not any more."[19] The
strong hatred which the son had felt for the father has surfaced as love. The
utter unscrupulousness and amorality have for a brief moment been
transformed into feeling and, therefore, into humanity.

The ironic ambivalence is underscored in the final words of the play in the form of a radio announcement that the president of American Electric, Mr. Mark Herries, would make a guest appearance to discuss the widely hunted swindler. Herries's comment "that to be absolutely powerful a man must first corrupt *himself* absolutely"[20] reflects Rattigan's skepticism about the possibility of any kind of redemption for the tycoon. In an interview Rattigan had said that *Ross* is about a man who wanted to be God and *Man and Boy* is about a man who wanted to be the devil.

Personal parallels obtrude on this modern morality play. Basil Anthony (like Ross of the previous drama, he has an assumed identity) is twenty-three years old and was born in 1911, the year of Rattigan's birth. At twenty-three Rattigan had made a break with his own father regarding a career choice. The time of the events in *Man and Boy* is 1934, two years before Rattigan's huge success with *French Without Tears*. Nearly thirty years later, Rattigan dramatizes the old myth of selling one's soul to the devil, feeling keenly in his own financial successes at the time the aspiring, idealistic boy he once was and the successful man he now is. As his last play before giving up the stage for the film world for the next seven years, *Man and Boy* seems an ironically fitting expression of his own state at the time. Further, Antonescu is from Rumania, where Frank Rattigan had spent some years as diplomat and which is drawn upon for characters in *The Sleeping Prince*. The mistresses of Antonescu, whom the American tycoon Herries described as the "most highly publicized mistresses of any man in the world—also a beautiful young wife"[21] suggest the women in Frank Rattigan's much-publicized affairs, already dramatized in *Who Is Sylvia?* Basil's financial problems as a struggling pianist were Rattigan's when he worked for Warner Brothers studio. The homosexual Herries and his young male friend who committed suicide are drawn from Rattigan's early experience. Autobiographical details are woven deftly into this play, which Michael Darlow sees as a parallel to Rattigan's possible reassessment of his own relationship to his father.[22]

Man and Boy is Rattigan's most pessimistic play. Like Shaw's *Heartbreak House,* Ibsen's *Wild Duck,* and Chekhov's *The Cherry Orchard,* there is a void at the center of things left by the cancellation of idealism by realism, youth by age, optimism by pessimism. In no other play of Rattigan's is the void so pronounced as in *Man and Boy.*

In varying ways, all of Rattigan's plays deal with internal and external conflicts of conscience, whether in the small man taking on the highest court in the land or in legendary heroes such as T. E. Lawrence and Sir Horatio Nelson in conflict with themselves. The succession of leading characters in Rattigan's work presents a varied pattern of the forms that battles of conscience take. The battle ends with some measure of victory, even though minuscule in a few instances. The victory for right in the case of Ronnie Winslow affected an entire nation. In Hester Collyer, Crocker-Harris, and Major Pollock, some measure of private dignity has been achieved, and in Rose Fish the mere presence of conscience in her final, fatal choice of Ron over the Kurt Masts of her life is a victory, however slim, of the needs of the individual over prevailing social pressures. However, Gregor Antonescu's success in disillusioning Basil about the last "lie" on which the financial empire had been built seems a prelude to his rejecting the son's love after an intense but brief expression of that love. The lies and rejections are major components in relationships between Rose and her daughter Fiona, between Crocker-Harris and his wife, between Major Pollock and the outside world, but nowhere is their consequence so total as in *Man and Boy*. Even though the father has sold his soul to the devil, the son can love him. Yet there is his troubling promise to Antonescu never to let the truth make him (Basil) cry.

The possibility of redemption for the man seems minuscule indeed, as Gregor's truth is that of a man who has rejected conscience and knowingly continues to reject it. Basil's ability to love even a father who has tried to become the devil is the ultimate attempt to keep Gregor's connection with humanity. Love is offered and rejected. The moral and emotional wasteland of Gregor seems unrelieved. Yet in this moral desert Rattigan's narrative power, Bernard Levin wrote, fuses with his dramatic cunning and his "imaginative curiosity about the springs of human activity—hot and glowing into his finest work and a play that outdistances all but a handful of authors writing in England today."[23]

Negative reactions to the play were strong, however. Because of the homosexual matter and the absence of psychological explanation for Gregor's actions, some criticism was quite harsh. Yet, one can argue, psychological explanations are not the terms of Rattigan's dramatic style. To expect the patterned motivations of Ibsenian or Strindbergian characters is to ignore those terms, which are the revelation of character through narrative means.

As Rattigan's wasteland play, *Man and Boy* lacks the questioning whose end is the self-knowledge of the previous plays. The question asked by a radio interviewer is put to Herries, himself of questionable moral cast. "Why did a man who, by 1929, had achieved every ambition that any great financier could hope for, a man who was already acclaimed. . . . Why did this man descend to . . . common swindling . . . and to total

ruin—both for himself and for millions of those who trusted him?"[24] The
answer is clearly dramatized throughout the play by Gregor's actions and
can be found in his two favorite words: liquidity and confidence.

The big confidence game, success, creates hero-worship, Gregor con-
tends, "but to be loved and worshipped by one's own boy—and by this boy
above all. . . . Oh, no. No. I will take almost any risk—you know that,
Sven—but not the risk of being so close to the pure in heart. 'And virtue
entered into him'—isn't that from the Bible?"[25] Underneath the hatred,
man and boy find that there is still love. But Gregor takes a step to the
point of no moral return to disillusion the boy, and he does succeed.
Neither man nor boy has any more questions, and it is left to the American
tycoon Herries to provide the expected, hypocritical answer to the question of the radio announcer.

John Russell Taylor regards *Man and Boy,* along with Coward's *A Song at
Twilight,* "as the first completely convincing, completely serious well-
made play in the British theatre for more than half a century. . . ."[26]
Taylor's assessment that the play is a distinct advance on *The Deep Blue
Sea,*[27] however, many would dispute. He continues that *Man and Boy*

for all its neatness as a piece of plotting . . . has the fascination of a tale that is
told, not precisely explicable, seeming to imply much more than it says. For
unlike *The Deep Blue Sea* it does not actually say anything: or what it has to say
escapes all neat, pat formulation. It is the character-portrait of a man without
qualities, and Rattigan seems in it for the first time to be moving outside the
neat, clear-cut world of the well-made play, where there is always an explanation
hidden somewhere in a secret drawer, and into the shifting, indeterminate world
of contemporary drama, which might take as its motto Gertrude Stein's sup-
posed last words "What is the answer . . . ? Very well then what is the
question?" But still preserving the form of the well-made play: a curious and
potentially explosive combination.[28]

With its intentionally limited run and despite some harsh reviews, *Man
and Boy* intrigues and fascinates with its conventional plotting of surface
action, its articulate dialogue and its near Beckettian sense of the void at
the center of things riding close to the surface features of the play. A
modern-day *Faust,* it is the third of Rattigan's stage dramas after 1956 and
the last stage production before his self-exile to the film world.

All three plays written after the Osborne explosion at the Royal Court
Theatre deal openly with homosexual subject matter. All three deal with
characters confronting the harsh realities of sex, confidence games, and

political and financial power. The inevitable consequences are relentlessly natural, particularly in *Ross* and *Man and Boy,* in which man aspires to be God in one and the devil in the other. As modern morality plays, the comment on the arts, politics, and finances is intertwined with painfully intimate experiences. A godlike Ross, a satanic Antonescu, and a totally human Rose Fish (embodying both the romantic and disillusioned in her very name) are indeed both representative types and distinctive individuals whose failures have only affirmed their respective strengths. The fragility and disguises of the characters in earlier plays now give way to power and honesty. The effects are noticeable in the very construction of the scenes in which tension-building debates and ironical situations deepen characterizations of people in whom separateness, community, and conscience still battle with each other in a fascinating blend of human activity. This trilogy of post-1956 plays, impressive each in its own way, is Rattigan's response to the challenge of the new waves of drama. In that response he has developed a direction that took him into seven years of writing for films and then into seven more years of stage activity in which he wrote three final plays.

Chapter Twelve

Stage Exile

Critical and Financial Considerations

The year in which *Man and Boy* premiered, 1963, marked the release of the film *The V.I.P.s,* for whose script Rattigan was paid more than forty thousand pounds (about eighty thousand dollars).[1] Called "a superb essay in glossy living" by Brigid Brophy in the *New Statesman,* the film was further described as "a superpackaged box of chocolates . . . [which] can with a little manipulation be enjoyed without nauseating or smearing you."[2] Expressing his own feelings about the mixed reactions to *Man and Boy* Rattigan said that although he had minded the bad notices, they had been kinder than expected. "I did not write *Man and Boy* to be successful. I am trying to get them to take me seriously as a writer."[3] In regard to *The V.I.P.s*'s notices, Rattigan said that since he was too old to write potboilers for the theater, they would now go to the films.[4] "They are easier to write and make more money. I do not have to earn my living now."[5] His comments reflect an ongoing conflict with certain critics who would not take him seriously. And his sense of injury was frequently expressed in comments like "You see—whisper it not to *Sight and Sound*—I actually ENJOYED *Grand Hotel, Dinner at Eight* and many other such products of Hollywood in its prime. I don't say they were better films than *Last Year in Marienbad*—although I'll bet that baffled even *Sight and Sound* a bit, too—I just say they were more enjoyable films."[6]

So for the remainder of the 1960s Rattigan's reputation settled as a writer of glossy, entertaining, escapist films. "My profession is described on my passport as 'dramatist,' and not as would be more accurate as 'writer' or playwright, screen-writer and occasional television writer.' Simply as 'dramatist.'"[7] Rattigan, simply, could not hide his hurt.

The V.I.P.s and *The Yellow Rolls-Royce*

The V.I.P.s is a variation of the "Grand Hotel" genre. Four stories are related about characters who have little in common except that they are all

114

running away from or to something and that they are all stranded by fog at Heathrow Airport. Earlier Rattigan had used this framework in *Flare Path* and in his major play, *Separate Tables*. Like so much of his work, this film features major actors of the time: Richard Burton, Elizabeth Taylor, Orson Welles, Margaret Rutherford, Maggie Smith.

Characters and thematic concerns of earlier plays and films stand out. The tractor-company tycoon here is a variation of Gregor Antonescu in *Man and Boy*; Paul Andros, the shipping millionaire, suggests Hester Collyer's steady, reliable, successful judge-husband; his wife, like Hester, has more basic sexual needs which drive her to elopement with a parasitic Frenchman whose character and financial status leave something to be desired. The main characters in each of the four stories have personal, professional, or corporate problems, which in the course of the fog-caused flight delay are resolved with varying degrees of success, including the Duchess of Brighton, whose uneasiness on her first flight won rave reviews in the performance by Margaret Rutherford.

Rattigan's lifelong romance with airplanes dating back to his World War II experiences and to early dramas and films such as *Flare Path* and *Sound Barrier* is updated in this film about modern jet travel. The film brings together once more the trio of Anatole de Grunwald (producer), Anthony Asquith (director), and Rattigan, whose film association started in *French Without Tears* in 1939 and continued through the World War II years and the postwar period.

A second major film of the 1960s, *The Yellow Rolls-Royce,* major in the sense of Hollywood-style spectacle, was released in 1965, two years after *The V.I.P.s.* Again the Asquith, de Grunwald, and Rattigan trio produced a lavish film, but this time clearly less substantive than its predecessor. And again the film consists of several tales; in each, a couple—a gangster's moll and her Italian gigolo, a marquess and her lover, a millionairess and a Yugoslav partisan—engage in their amours in the luxury of a Rolls-Royce. The star-studded cast includes Rex Harrison, Jeanne Moreau, Shirley MacLaine, Alain Delon, George C. Scott, Ingrid Bergman, Omar Sharif, and Art Carney.

Among the spectacular settings there is a "grotto covering an area of 16,000 square feet. Under the floor of the set was a tank filled with 100,000 gallons of water heated to a temperature of 80 degrees."[8] The action takes place in England, France, Sweden, Egypt, and the United States. Everything about the film is Hollywood glamour at its grandest, and it pretends to nothing more than just that. "Let us bring a little glamour into the drabness of their lives, you can hear its makers saying, as they set before us, with a flourish of *largesse,* individual portions of flyblown trifle. Authentic glamour in the cinema is a rare commodity: a difficult, secret blend of elegance, opulence, charm and wit, achieved sometimes in Paris and Hollywood, but never in Britain, where it usually means yet another dose of second-hand Herbert Wilcox."[9] Kenneth Tynan's criticism included the suggestion that the film should have been completely Americanized. Derek Hill in the *Sunday Telegraph* described it as a "sumptuous vehicle, star-studded, gold-plated, shock-proof. And probably critic-proof, too." For "when so many multi-million extravaganzas merely bore, there is little point in challenging a blockbuster which actually avoids dullness."[10] Glamorous and glossy as they are, these are but two films in a long list of impressive cinema credits that augment Rattigan's stage reputation.

Many of their subjects parallel those of his stage plays and have their origins in the 1930s, when, struggling to make ends meet, Rattigan was employed by Warner Brothers as a script writer at their Teddington Studios earning forty-five pounds by his seventh year. One of the ironies of his studio employment was that he had offered the company *Gone Away,* an earlier title for *French Without Tears,* but the script had been returned as "no good, either as a film or a play."[11] Although humiliated by severe criticism from his studio superiors, Rattigan later acknowledged the value of learning that "there was no time for frills. The plot had to be told in three lines."[12]

Screen Versions of Stageplays

Rattigan had the satisfaction of seeing many of his stage dramas filmed successfully. Among the critical and financial successes in this group are *French Without Tears* (1939), *While the Sun Shines* (1947), *The Winslow Boy* (1948), *The Browning Version* (1951), *The Deep Blue Sea* (1955), *The Prince and the Showgirl* (1957), *Separate Tables* (1958), and *A Bequest to the Nation* (1973).

World War II Films

A second group of his films have been praised as some of the finest motion pictures about World War II, particularly those dealing with the Royal Air Force. In 1942 two films were released. The first, *The Day Will Dawn,* written with de Grunwald from a story by Frank Owen about the Nazi invasion of Norway, was retitled *The Avengers* in America. Featuring Ralph Richardson, Deborah Kerr, Roland Culver, Griffith Jones, and

Francis L. Sullivan, with Hugh Williams in the leading role, it is the story of a journalist who finds himself entangled into guiding bombers to a U-boat base. After his return to England, he continues his anti-Nazi activities until the day will dawn for victory.

Uncensored, the second of the 1942 films, was written in collaboration with Rodney Ackland from Wolfgang Whilhelm's adaptation of Oscar E. Millard's book. Eric Portman and Peter Glenville drew strong notices for their performances in this story about a secret newspaper in Nazi-occupied Belgium. Both films are generally regarded as proficient war films with the propagandistic war heroism so necessary to the English during the dark days of the Battle of Britain.

In *Journey Together* (1945), Rattigan's writing about the war continued. Commissioned by the Royal Air Force as inspiration to recruits, the film documentary was produced on location in various training bases in England and America. Flight Lieutenants Rattigan and Boulting, writer and director, respectively, were highly praised, as were the sensitive performances of Richard Attenborough and Edward G. Robinson.

But the war film of Rattigan's which received widest and warmest acclaim is *The Way to the Stars* (retitled in America *Johnny in the Clouds*), also a 1945 release. Bosley Crowther in the *New York Times* described it as "a wistful reflection upon a grim and tragic period in British life, a period of untold grief and suffering but of spiritual experience, too. And it is this sense of spiritual experience which is most elevating in the film."[13] With changes in characters and situation, the film is based on Rattigan's first recognized serious play, *Flare Path.* Michael Redgrave and John Mills offered splendid performances, and Trevor Howard and Jean Simmons were introduced in the film. Asquith, de Grunwald, and Rattigan, in still another joint production, received solid praise for this poignant drama of British and American airmen at a bomber station in Britain.

Other films, not directly about World War II but drawn from life during that period, included *English Without Tears* (American title, *Her Man Gilbey*) and *Quiet Wedding.* The latter, an adaptation of Esther McCracken's stage play, was interrupted in its filming by German bombing.

In all, Rattigan's demand as a screen writer before his first critically acclaimed play, *The Winslow Boy,* in 1946 was most impressive. His film reputation intact, Rattigan in 1952 earned additional laurels from the by-now classic *Breaking Through the Sound Barrier* (American retitling of *The Sound Barrier*). As an "uncommonly literate and sensitive original script by Terence Rattigan, [it] is a wonderfully beautiful and thrilling comprehension of the power of jet airplanes and of the minds and emotions of the people who are involved with these miraculous machines. And it is played with consummate revelation of subtle and profound characters by a cast headed by Ralph Richardson, Nigel Patrick and Ann Todd."[14] William Whitebait wrote that "*The Sound Barrier* reinstates him; more, it proves that, given the right subject, he can exercise a passionate skill rare indeed in English film-making. But who could have guessed, looking at his record, that he would find this subject in jet propulsion? . . . Well, there it is; and *The Sound Barrier* will enthrall audiences everywhere as has no English film since *The Third Man*."[15]

Briefly the story is of a young woman who finds it difficult to understand the obsession of her father, husband, various engineers, test pilots, etc., with the development of the jet plane to the point of fanatic absorption with this newest challenge of the future. Eventually she does develop some understanding of the men who can calmly listen to a dead test pilot's radioed report as he crashes. Machine and man are dramatized as a challenge to each other, and in their eventual union is realized one of the most sublime experiences of man. Rattigan's superb scene construction was called attention to over and over in the reviews for the tautness and tension-creating excitement that reached heights of exaltation. The film enjoys frequent showings on television, and time has not lessened its sense of the exciting challenge of the unknown.

Rattigan's films, like his plays, are a chronicle of the events and moods of rapidly changing decades of the twentieth century. They reflect his deepening view of human involvement in those events, the involvement of historical personages sometimes, but for the most part of the average person.

As early as 1941, his scripted *Quiet Wedding* deals with the "uncertainties that crowd the mind of a girl who, wanting a quiet wedding, is forced by family pride into a lavish ceremony and is completely unnerved by the gruelling grind of preparing her trousseau." The *New York Times* review concluded with a comment on the charm of the film, whose component parts "are as delicately balanced as the mechanism of a watch."[16]

English Without Tears (1944) is a variation, as its title implies, of the stage play *French Without Tears*. This time, however, the language school is conducted for Allied officers in England. The comedy, with Michael Wilding, Lilli Palmer, Margaret Rutherford, and Roland Culver, retains the situational humor and wittiness of the earlier play, as perhaps only the English really know how to laugh at themselves.

Cinematic Variety

Two 1948 films offer strong contrasts in mood and subject matter. One, *Brighton Rock* (retitled *Young Scarface*), written in collaboration with Graham Greene from Greene's novel, brought together the successful team of Rattigan, director John Boulting, and actor Richard Attenborough, who had earlier won plaudits for *Journey Together*. About gang warfare in Brighton, the film received mixed reviews, the *New York Times* critic calling it a mixture of the sordid and the sublime. The second of the films, *Bond Street*, with its Rattiganesque style of employing several tales, was written with Rodney Ackland and Anatole de Grunwald. The four stories deal with the lives of ordinary people as they are variously affected by the wedding preparations of a young lady of wealth and social standing. Like its predecessor, *Quiet Wedding*, its reception was mild. But the multinarrative structure anticipates later film styles already discussed in regard to *The V.I.P.s* and *The Yellow Rolls-Royce*.

Rattigan's concern with the man-and-boy theme at this point in his career began to emerge as a central theme, and it found expression in another subject of lifelong interest to him: cricket. *The Final Test,* successfully televised and then later filmed, received praise from literary and nonliterary critics alike. Its subject is the final test match, the English equivalent of World Series baseball in the United States. An aging cricketer playing his final match wants his son to attend the event. The son, an aspiring writer, prefers to "meet a hero of his own, a poet and playwright, rather than watch his father's historic last innings."[17] During his own schooldays, Rattigan was constantly divided between his interests in cricket and the theater, and like the young man of the play, he was divided from his father on the matter of a career choice.

Gratified by the success of both television and film versions, Rattigan in an interview said that his story was of a "sports hero who was as intolerant of his poet son as the latter was disinterested in his parent's preoccupation. Selecting cricket, England's national sport, for the background only served to bring the comic conflict into glaring relief."[18]

He was especially pleased that the *Times* critic noted that "Mr. Rattigan even contrives to make his subject yield a little dissertation on creative and noncreative artists."[19]

The Final Test anticipates the father-son conflict in *Man and Boy* and *In Praise of Love*. In the latter, particularly, the parallels are close, as the son, an aspiring playwright, experiences a father's negligence in attending his son's television debut. It, too, contains a dissertation on creative artists. The year 1955 saw the release of *The Man Who Loved Redheads,* an adaptation of *Who Is Sylvia?* with Roland Culver, John Justin, Gladys Cooper, and Denholm Elliott. The film features Moira Shearer, famed ballerina, playing all four major feminine roles, and its reviews ranged from "enjoyable" to "captivating."

The ten drafts which Rattigan wrote for the 1969 musical film version of *Goodbye Mr. Chips* were "enough to put me off writing filmscripts for life,"[20] he admitted to Philip Oakes. He had been living in Bermuda and Paris and was glad to get back to England for the royal premiere of the film. Laboring over the script must have affected him strongly, for he recalled in an interview with Louise Sweeney his working for fifteen pounds a week at Warner Brothers back in the 1930s, "a bruising but a useful" experience.[21] During the writing for this film he underwent a serious appendectomy that brought him close to death.

In the 1960s Rattigan completed the screenplay for *Lawrence of Arabia,* which for a variety of reasons was never filmed. Instead, Robert Bolt's script was used several years later. But the writing of the script served Rattigan well as the basis for his stageplay *Ross.*

Television and Radio Plays

Augmenting his writing for the screen, a series of scripts for television and radio reflect the versatility of Rattigan's art. In addition to *The Final Test,* already discussed, *Ninety Years On* (about Winston Churchill) was aired in 1964. *Nelson,* televised in 1966, later developed into *A Bequest to the Nation.* For his much-admired actress friend Margaret Leighton, Rattigan wrote *All on Her Own,* shown in 1968. In 1972, *High Summer,* a play written twenty-five years earlier as a third piece to go with *The Browning Version* and *Harlequinade,* was sent to "Armchair Theatre" in response to a request for rejected or little-known plays. Even with Margaret Leighton and Roland Culver, however, it turned out to be only minimally successful, *Nijinsky,* another television play, still awaits production. Rattigan's radio play *Cause Célèbre,* aired in 1972, became the basis for his final stage play in 1977.

Heart to Heart

Standing out among his television dramas is *Heart to Heart,* the only nonstage work included in his *Collected Plays.* Seen in 1964, it is ahead of its time in a satiric treatment of a flawed politician, Sir Stanley Johnson, and an idolized but flawed interviewer, David Mann, who hopes to bring the politician down by exposure of sexual and bribery scandal. The play reads uncannily like the David Frost–Richard Nixon interviews conducted more than a decade later. In spite of echoes of the American scene such as the politician's emotional plea to his public, the use of a cat which the politician privately hated, the reference to a vicuña coat, the basis for the satire is English. The anti-intellectualism of the Sir Stanleys of the world and the false hominess of politicians are English as well as American. Rattigan's lifelong interest in politics and his familiarity with the American political scene, particularly the Joseph McCarthy era in the 1950s, when people and careers were destroyed, are echoed in this play about an English politician and a TV interviewer.

Not surprisingly, conscience-ridden heroes similar to those in the plays of Ibsen and Arthur Miller experience the collision of private and public worlds. Interviewer and politician are flawed characters, David Mann by alcohol and Sir Stanley by a corrupt past. David succeeds in exposing and bringing down Sir Stanley, but in the process he, too, suffers. As Grand Inquisitor to Sir Stanley, his own vulnerabilities—an unsatisfying marriage and his alcoholism—are exposed, and he must compromise or give up money, position, and the purely sexual gratification of his marriage. In the end he chooses the latter course. Kenneth More's and Ralph Richardson's powerful performances were equal to Rattigan's compelling characterizations and the brilliant, hard-hitting dialogue.

David Mann is not much different from the earlier characters of Rattigan's dramas, but what occurs, interestingly, is that antagonist and protagonist reflect a balancing of successes and failures lacking in the earlier characters. The deepest ambivalences of people are fascinatingly exposed and sustained, rather than happily resolved.

When Rattigan returned to England for the premiere of *Goodbye Mr. Chips* in 1969, he was glad to get back to both country and stage. Self-exile became for both him and his critics, increasingly, a betrayal of a major talent for the glamorous and glossy film spectaculars of that period of his life.

Chapter Thirteen
Return to the Stage

When Rattigan returned to the English stage in 1970, he had been through a series of geographical and emotional dislocations. His increasing isolation and loneliness were noticeable. Once when ill in his luxurious Eaton Place flat, he had only his recently acquired secretary to nurse him through the bank-holiday weekend. His earlier bout with an illness falsely diagnosed as leukemia and his shuttling among Ischia, Hollywood, and Paris for health and tax reasons contributed to the loneliness. During the 1960s, while writing for the musical remake of *Goodbye Mr. Chips* in Naples, Rattigan had undergone an emergency appendectomy, coming close to death because of unsanitary medical facilities.

At the same time, his extravagant life-style, symbolized by Rolls-Royces, included lavish entertaining. Elizabeth Taylor and Richard Burton during their much-publicized liaison while filming *Cleopatra* were among his friends. His more casual attitude toward publicity about his homosexual associations and the new freedoms of English life and the stage reflected a self-confidence and ease with hitherto disguised subjects.

Homes, flats, and villas at Sunningdale, Brighton, Eaton Place, Ischia, Paris, and Scotland became a way of life for him. His famous hospitality and extravagant life-style were enjoyed by many friends and acquaintances, including a few parasites genuinely disliked by his long-standing friends.

The other side of a glamorous life, however, provided counterpoint not visible except to his closest friends. As a tax exile, he was forced to be absent from England for a whole year. Even when his mother was sick— she was then in her seventies—he could be as close only as a telephone call from Paris. In addition, both of his own close encounters with death and his self-imposed, seven-year absence from the English stage took their toll.

122

A Bequest to the Nation

When he returned to the London stage with *A Bequest to the Nation* (1970), it was the third successive time he began a decade with a history play. And like his two previous history plays about Alexander the Great and T. E. Lawrence, *A Bequest to the Nation* is deliberately loose in the two stories it dramatizes. In one, the relationships among the members of Lord Nelson's family are explored; in the other, Nelson's tempestuous affair with his mistress, the convention-flouting Emma Hamilton, is developed.

Also, like *Ross*, which was written from an unproduced filmscript, *A Bequest to the Nation* is an adaptation of a television play, *Nelson: A Portrait in Miniature*, written at the suggestion of the Duke of Edinburgh, as a means of raising funds to restore a sailing ship, the *Cutty Sark*. It is the second of Rattigan's occasional plays, the first being *The Sleeping Prince*, written for the coronation of Queen Elizabeth. Rattigan, who long had been thinking of a drama about Nelson, was having problems about writing about a successful figure. It was Prince Philip who finally suggested one intriguing aspect of the Nelson story: why hadn't England granted Nelson's request that his mistress be provided for after his death? She was his final bequest to the nation, and the nation had generously provided for the other members of his family. There must have been something in the character of Emma to preclude the granting of this request. England's refusal to do so was Nelson's one major defeat. So Emma's coarse, cowlike character and her flagrant disregard for the public in her social behavior became the basis of Rattigan's story and his characterization of two of England's most written about historical figures.

Historical events in the play function as a catalyst for the dramatization of the Ladies Hamilton and Nelson, for as forceful a character as Nelson is, especially in his deeply ambivalent feelings about personal desire and public duty, the characters of the two women remain poignantly steadfast even in the final scene, after Nelson's death, when they meet for the first and final time in a confrontation that in its untheatrical, unsentimentalized way is one of Rattigan's most moving and most realistic endings. It is they who finally remain on center stage in the spectator's mind.

The themes of the drama are familiar. The father-son conflict in this case involves George Matcham, Lord Nelson's nephew, who finds his public-school values challenged by the behavior of his famous uncle. For him the initiation rites into adulthood become painful as Nelson's cruelty toward his wife and his obsession with his mistress disillusion young George. Compounding this disillusionment is George's discovery of the nepotism involved in the positions which various members of Nelson's family hold. Both man and boy experience conflicts of conscience which are resolved by death in the first instance and departure for school in the second.

Another theme, probably the major one, is the compulsive sexual and emotional need of a public idol whose socially approved marriage does not fulfill that need. Consequently, the private and public humiliations, similar to those of Crocker-Harris and Hester Collyer earlier, become matters of national interest. But Nelson's private guilt may be the strongest of his humiliations. For, even though he has disavowed his wife, he is tortured by her persistently unselfish attitude toward him. Although she knows that she cannot satisfy his sexual needs as can Emma Hamilton, she is patient and generous.

A third closely related theme is the problem of choice. The events leading up to that choice in a devastatingly cumulative fashion heighten the narrative and create the dramatic tensions of the play. In opposition to the wishes of his family, for example, George chooses not to break his promise to his aunt and delivers an all-important letter from her to Nelson. Similarly, after consultations with his staff and subsequent to the reading of his letter from his wife, Nelson, opposing general opinion, chooses to conduct the Trafalgar venture personally in full naval uniform, making him an easy target for the enemy. His decision is made with full knowledge of the possible consequences. Conscience and duty in boy and man win painful moral and emotional victories like those of the average persons in earlier plays.

The structure of *A Bequest to the Nation* continues the two-act tradition of *Adventure Story* and *Ross*. In Act I, the exposition of Nelson's family background with its conflicts takes on a life of its own. Nelson's sister, brother-in-law, and nephew, Kitty and George Matcham and George, Jr., appear to serve as context for the Nelson-Hamilton story. But their own situation, with young George and Lady Nelson as its focus, is a drama in its own right. Lady Nelson, called "Tom Tit" by the family because of her birdlike walk, finally succeeds in having a conversation with young George and even extracts a promise from him to deliver her letter to Lord Nelson. Since Nelson wanted it that way, the family had succeeded up to this time in avoiding any contact with Lady Nelson.

In Act II, a series of discussions between Nelson and his staff regarding the conduct of the war are gradually interwoven with big scenes in which Emma, as Nelson's hostess, entertains at Merton, his official residence. In each scene her drinking becomes heavier, her language coarser, and her actions more disgusting, until at one point she insults publicly even the king whom Nelson serves. The contrast between her and the well-bred, sensitive Lady Nelson could hardly be sharper.

The contrast is accented by Nelson's explanation to Captain Hardy, who serves as a surrogate conscience to both Nelson and Emma. Nelson talks of the shame that he feels "nearly every day that I spend at Emma's side,"[1] but then of the nights that make up for those days. For "without the bed what would it be? Nothing. But that other love—that ineffable bliss of wedlock—the one so blessed by my father and thought by all the world so fitting for a national hero; the right brave smile, the rigid body the—'if this makes my beloved husband happy then I'll do it, even if the messy business quite disgusts my well-bred sensibilities.'"[2]

The final scene occurs between Emma and Frances after Nelson's death. The gentility of Nelson's wife shows in her willingness to implement Nelson's vow to have Emma Hamilton provided for after his death. Emma, in a drunken stupor, refuses that aid. Both women maintain their pride as Emma's bottle of brandy spills slowly to the floor and Frances "hobbles her birdlike way into darkness."[3] Both demonstrate an oft-recurring Rattigan theme, here contained in earlier words of Lord Minto to Lady Frances: ". . . hope can only mean despair, and if you could kill the one you could also kill the other."[4] Nelson's death at Trafalgar and the respective conditions of his wife and mistress for the rest of their lives, one in emotional and the other in financial poverty, illustrate this devastating truth. Yet the strength of the two women to go on, their respective integrities intact, is affirmative of the human spirit.

Young George's journey from innocence to experience begins with his finding out that his family had been given various positions at Nelson's request. More importantly, his aunt's story awakens in him a curiosity about Uncle Horatio's hatred of his wife. It is a question which, although answered later by Nelson, is not understood by George.

In explaining human love and human hatred, Nelson talks about "an enemy who won't retaliate." "Who answers every broadside with a signal gently fluttering at the mast which says: 'Whatever you do to me, my dearest husband, I will always forgive you and go on loving you for ever.' What about that enemy, George? In this matter of loving enemies my dearest wife has beat me in the chase. What is there, then, left for me but to hate?"[5]

George finds himself caught among the various conflicts: personal, familial, military. For the more important plot involving Nelson and

Emma Hamilton, George serves as a go-between, and his delivery of his
aunt's letter, which had been returned in the mail by Emma and had,
consequently, been unread by Nelson, catalyzes events, especially Emma's
outlandish behavior and Nelson's final decision to participate personally in
full dress in the Trafalgar naval battle. But with his departure for public
school, George's story is a complete one, in which innocence has been
sullied by experience. His famous uncle's problem, that of dealing with an
experience that cannot lightly dismiss the guilt by which it is accom-
panied, continues until his death. Nelson's victory is military; George's is
a moral one; those of Lady Nelson and Lady Hamilton are personal.

Rattigan's lifelong concern with conventionally approved marriages,
yet deeply unfulfilling ones, nowhere receives such searing treatment as in
this play. Conscience and duty on the one hand and sexual passion on the
other create and maintain complex, ambivalent loyalties that characters
cannot resolve with any finality or much satisfaction, but they can and do
make choices in full knowledge of the consequences of those choices. They
are aware, and they act out of that awareness. Most of all, they continue to
live. Only when history and facts dictate does Rattigan allow his characters
the conventional endings of suicide or death. So Lord Nelson dies in battle,
and the women continue to live in their respective styles.

Honest in his dramatization of famous historical figures, Rattigan
created fiction from known fact by exploring the possibilities of the
complex and diverse human dimensions of his characters. The basis for his
dramatic version of the Nelson-Hamilton legend is the possibility that
Emma may have been the cowlike figure he depicts and that in her nature
may lie at least part of the reason that the English nation refused this last
request of Nelson's while granting all others so very generously. It is,
however, only a possibility, just as earlier, in *Ross,* Rattigan dramatized
the possibility that Lawrence may have enjoyed the homosexual rape by the
Turks. In both plays, sexual passion, in repressed, sublimated, or realized
forms, is crucial to the characters and the plots. Antagonistic to the
driving sexual passion are conscience, duty, and civilized sensibilities,
sometimes merely social respectability. The resolution of the nature-
nurture conflict is made only by the protagonist, who finally, as an
individual, must determine what is right and then see that right is done.
The ultimate importance of the individual, whether he be an average
schoolboy like Ronnie Winslow or an idolized national hero like Lord
Nelson, is primary.

In addition to its television and stage versions, in 1966 and 1970,
respectively, the Nelson story continued its life in still another form, the

film, released in 1973. One of the interesting coincidences of the film version, as well as Glenda Jackson's self-criticism of her own fitness for the part of Lady Hamilton, is the playing of the role of George Matcham by young Dominic Guard, who also played a curiously similar role as go-between in Harold Pinter's screen adaptation of Hartley's novel *The Go-Between.* Just as the frustrated, genteel characters of Rattigan's plays developed in Osborne's plays into the less genteel and very angry young men, there are in Rattigan's play about Nelson curious similarities to the sexual, social, and emotional ambivalences in the characters of Pinter, with differences, of course, of style, particularly the way in which Pinter fragments failures and frustration into puzzling enigmas. Rattigan frequently "took on" Osborne in a debate about the play of ideas and social commitment, but always expressed admiration for Pinter, with whom he had a friendship.

In Praise of Love; Before Dawn

Rattigan's second drama after his return to the London stage, *In Praise of Love,* belongs to the double-bill genre of *Playbill* and *Separate Tables.* One of the plays is a serious drama and the other a diversion. The order of performance was to be one "in which the insubstantial play followed the substantial and an audience, moved by the first," would be "reasonably diverted by the second."[6] In addition, as in the previous double bills, the same actors would perform in both plays. However, the curtain-raiser *Before Dawn,* preceded *After Lydia* at the Duchess Theatre in 1973—for Rattigan, an unfortunate order. A farcical reworking of the Tosca story by Sardou, *Before Dawn* was a brief disaster, causing a "deeply distressing" interval and raising for Sheridan Morley, the critic, a serious question about "staying for the other half of the bill."[7] Even the acting talents of Joan Greenwood and Donald Sinden did not redeem it.

As a parody of the theme of its companion play and as a parody of the well-made play techniques, Rattigan adapted both the techniques and plot of Sardou with a mixture of farce and seriousness that produces a certain awkwardness. Tosca's consistent "attitudes," as though life imitated opera style, are awkward when compared to the straightforward manner of Scarpia in matters of physical passion. It is Rattigan's only play in which the obviously contrived Scribean techniques, such as secrets known to the audience but withheld from certain characters, a trivial object such as a handkerchief, or misunderstandings and the consequent teeter-totter action of superficial suspense, etc., are employed in the

prescribed tradition of Scribe and Sardou. It was received as the worst of
Rattigan's plays.

Yet it is interesting for several reasons. Rattigan takes the well-made
plot and uses its mechanically contrived devices to parody itself. The
trivial object on which a complicated intrigue would eventually turn is a
handkerchief whose dropping would be a signal to Scarpia's officer that he
should take certain actions in regard to the execution of Tosca's lover
Mario. Such signals frequently misfire or are misunderstood, and from
such misunderstandings the complications develop. There are coincidences and twists and turns of the plot that create superficial suspense.
Normally, these constitute the total action and purpose of the play. Here,
however, they are used long enough to get Tosca into Scarpia's bed. Scarpia
is shamed by his impotence with Tosca, and for the remaining portion of
the play he debates with Tosca the merits of physical and platonic love. In
the end Tosca's physical needs give in, and she and Scarpia realize their
physical passion for each other. Realism and parody unite, if somewhat
awkwardly.

There are some familiar touches in the drama, as in the references to
Emma Hamilton, who is held in high regard by the Italian royal family. In
addition, the melodramatic behavior of Tosca, as though her life were an
opera, recalls the "attitudes" of Emma Hamilton in her entertainments as
Nelson's hostess at Merton. A well-known diva, Tosca lacks the coarseness
of Emma, yet her physical passion is strong enough in their first encounter
to render Scarpia impotent. It was not until their many conversations and
their discovery of mutually political methods that Scarpia's impotence
disappears and they are able to consummate their desires on equal terms, a
touch Rattigan adds to the story.

In the setting of the drama, Rattigan has returned to the scene of his
early Harrovian play about Cesar Borgia, and in the story itself to his early
fascination with history.

In a different production and in Rattigan's intended order, *Before Dawn*
may prove to be the diverting contrast to *After Lydia* he intended.

In Praise of Love: After Lydia

After Lydia proved vastly different, in spite of the disastrous curtain-
raiser. With the same cast, especially Joan Greenwood's "performance of
stunning credibility" and the "universally excellent" support of Donald
Sinden, Richard Warwick, and Don Fellows, critical reaction turned
around completely. When the play was brought to New York, the

curtain-raiser was dropped, and *After Lydia* was retitled *In Praise of Love,* with some changes mostly involving lengthening of the drama.

In Praise of Love dramatizes the psychological and emotional handling of a terminal illness, a subject with which Rattigan had had some intimate experience. He had lived with Rex Harrison and Kay Kendall in California while the latter was dying of leukemia. His own false alarm with leukemia and then his Italian appendectomy had affected him strongly. Ironically, even as *In Praise of Love* was being performed in New York in 1974, with Rex Harrison and Julie Harris, Rattigan was shortly to face another diagnosis, this time an accurate one: cancer of the bone marrow.

In the four-character play, Sebastian Cruttwell, a novelist turned critic, is married to Lydia, an Estonian refugee whom he had married in Berlin after World War II, with the mutual intention of divorce after she was resettled in England. However, the birth of their son Joey changed that intention. Joey is now twenty, and his first play is to be shown the next day on British television. A third writer and a family friend, Mark Walters (Marcus Waldt), a successful Lithuanian-American novelist, visits the Cruttwell household. Long in love with Lydia, he can discuss serious matters with her honestly and freely. Like Joan in *After the Dance,* Lydia finds expression of emotion difficult with her husband but very easy with Mark. Rattigan's characterization of Lydia is deepened and made complex by its sharp focus on Lydia's cancer. Joan's emotional frustration in the earlier play had no clear focus, but consisted, rather, of a pervasive boredom and sense of uselessness.

Sebastian deals with the knowledge of Lydia's condition by hiding from her the fact that he knows its seriousness. His way of hiding his knowledge is to avoid at all costs any display of emotion, any solicitous behavior, or any indication of an unusual situation. Their surface behavior consists of playing witty games about trivial and serious matters alike: the disorderly arrangement of his books, the political activism of their son, whose new liberalism is centrist rather than the old-Stalinist left of Sebastian, the prostitute's life which Lydia engaged in for sheer survival during the Russian occupation of Estonia. Indeed, Lydia has developed some of Sebastian's verbal game-playing as a defensive strategy.

As she confides in Mark, we find that she has been rifling the files of her doctor to keep up with the results of the tests she is constantly taking. Not until her conversations with Mark does she find out that Sebastian knows all. Sebastian's confidences to Mark have disclosed that the hatbox on a top shelf of a bookcase, reached only by extension of the ladder, is the hiding place for medical diagnoses Sebastian has been receiving from the doctor and hiding from Lydia. This small piece of Scribean carpentry, for the well-made play depends on some small object as a means of withholding and revealing secrets at crucial moments in the play, is integrated with realistic credibility in the series of conversations between Lydia and Sebastian, Lydia and Mark, Mark and Sebastian, and to a lesser degree between Joey and his parents.

With each of the conversational duets, the games accumulate a tension until, on a small pretext, Sebastian's seeming lack of feeling for his son on the occasion of the latter's television premiere causes emotions to explode. When Sebastian fails to show up for the viewing of his son's play, Lydia, angered to the breaking point over her husband's failure to join the celebration, delivers two physical blows to him when he finally puts in an appearance. Her frustration finds release in Mark's confidence and finally in this physical confrontation.

Confidante to Lydia, Mark serves the same function for Sebastian, who reveals his all-out effort to conceal his real emotion and the truth from Lydia and Joey. He also tells Mark how Lydia escaped from Nazi mass shootings by timing her falling down just seconds before the storm troopers fired. She had survived only by pretending death and by having been reported dead. Very unsentimentally Sebastian admits that his present torture lies in the fact that he had not realized that he really loved her until he had found out about her impending death. Her earlier pretense of death and his current pretense of ignorance create ironic realities.

Sebastian has managed to hide the pain by "transforming emotion into huffiness," using both Joey and Lydia as a punching bag. And in one angry cry, he utters what for Rattigan was a lifelong attitude toward the repressed emotions of the English: "Do you know what 'le vice Anglais?'—the English vice—really is? Not flagellation, not pederasty—whatever the French believe it to be. It's our refusal to admit to our emotions. We think they demean us, I suppose."[8]

Earlier Lydia had confessed to Mark that Sebastian had reproved her for parading her emotions publicly. Her own feelings are reflected in the emotional communication she can have only with Mark. "Oh damn the English! Sometimes I think that their bad form doesn't just lie in revealing their emotions, it's in having any at all."[9] The overriding insistence in Rattigan's dramas is the humanizing quality of emotions and the freedom to express them, whatever form of socially disapproved behavior that expression takes, whether it is a schoolmaster's emotional breakdown, a

Hester Collyer's obsession with a shiftless ex-flyer, a Major Pollock's sexual deviations in dark theaters.

However, the difference between the situation of Lydia and Sebastian and that of earlier Rattigan characters is that for once there is an equality of sorts between two equally respectable, middle-class characters. At this point in their marriage they are equally intelligent, socially compatible, and they reach an understanding of each other not realized in the characters of preceding plays. Yet, even when the disguises have been exposed, understood, and accepted, they are once more resumed, as Sebastian and his hostile son sit down to a game of chess and Lydia slowly disappears up the stairs. But with the resumption of the normal pattern of behavior, there is a change which understanding brings to that pattern. Lydia will die, and the three men will face life without her. The finality of "never, never, never, never, never," Lear's words which Rattigan has used in several plays, remains with Sebastian. This finality counterpoints sharply and dissonantly the game-playing avoidance of emotion.

In addition to the theme of emotional repression, several other of Rattigan's dramatic themes are recognizable. The father-son hostility is especially strong, but with Lydia's impending death and the gained understanding on the part of all the characters, its intensity has diminished. In an inversion of a situation in *The Final Test* in which the son chooses not to attend his father's last cricket match, it is the father who for complex reasons does not join the celebration of Joey's first television play. Their separateness even in political attitudes—the old liberalism of Sebastian and the new centrist politics of Joey—further sharpens their differences, but in a discussion of the differences, an understanding between the two is begun.

The play is also about the creative writer and about art. Sebastian is a novelist turned sour and turned critic; Mark, the financially successful novelist, is not seriously affected by the accusation of commercialism aimed at him by Sebastian. Joey is of the new generation of writers, getting his start by writing plays for television. The three in their ways reflect views on new and old art aired in Chekhov's *The Seagull*, a play about a popular, experienced author and a young, very idealistic writer.

All of the themes, however, are permeated with a mellowness and a sense of balanced perspective, possibly as Rattigan himself has mellowed. In domestic relations, art, and politics, Rattigan is an eloquent spokesman for the refined sensibility of an earlier time, and Sebastian is, perhaps, as one critic has put it, a "massive defense of all the things his generation expected of their contemporaries—exquisite taste and mental elegance and a refusal to tell the truth if the truth would hurt, in short all the beliefs that are no longer very trendy."[10]

In this, his penultimate play, Rattigan has not only incorporated his major themes but has done so with a miniaturist elegance of scene construction, whose ironies and subtle unspoken truths suggest increasingly the indirectness of Chekhov. For example, as Mark generously presents the chess set to Sebastian, the mink jacket to Lydia, and the cufflinks to Joey, his actions contrast sharply with the absence of such external and material show of emotion in Sebastian. Yet it is Sebastian who many years ago had made the supremely generous gesture in Berlin and who in his upper-class English fashion continued that generous, if unspoken, spirit. When he recounts to Mark the horrors of Lydia's experience with Nazi brutality and with her subsequent survival under the Russians as a prostitute, he reflects in the deepest sense a caring husband. Similarly, Lydia's proposed vacation with Mark is her ploy to express her deep, unexpressed love for Sebastian so that after her death father and son would have some basis on which to grow closer and so that Sebastian can be taken care of. Both Lydia and Sebastian are equally strong characters and act out of their strengths with a delicacy and finesse possible only by implicit means.

Finally, *In Praise of Love* belongs to an increasingly popular dramatic genre dealing with psychological problems created by terminal illnesses in families. *A Day in the Death of Joe Egg* and *National Health* by Peter Nichols; more recently, the British play *Whose Life Is It Anyway?;* and in America *Cold Storage, The Shadow Box,* and *Wings* have made a strong impact on the modern stage. Rattigan himself witnessed a television production of *In Praise of Love,* even as he was dying of cancer.

Cause Célèbre

His last stageplay and the third after his return to England, *Cause Célèbre,* fittingly concludes a long career of a distinguished dramatist. Viewed by some as the most autobiographical of his plays, it contains a subplot or, more accurately, a coplot which parallels rather closely his early schoolboy initiation into sexual experience and the attitudes of parents who were responsible for their son's ignorance and, consequently, the emotional and physical damage suffered. Like Rattigan's own father, Mr. Davenport, Tony's father, causes domestic problems with his mistress-prone life-style. Socially condoned sexual attitudes which result in hypocrisy and injury are attacked by Rattigan more strongly than in any previous drama. The fictional drama is woven with that of a famous 1935 English court case involving Alma Rattenbury and her young lover, renamed George Wood in the play.

Rattigan had already written *The Winslow Boy*, based on a case of nationwide interest early in the century; the Alma Rattenbury case, however, was one which he followed closely in the middle 1930s as it was reported in the newspapers. Its dramatic possibilities had stayed with him and grown over the forty intervening years. Like Ronnie Winslow, Alma Rattenbury had captivated the attention of the whole nation, but for vastly different reasons. It was the first time in English legal history that two defendants in a murder case, tried at the same time, lied in order to save the other person. In addition, the most intimate sexual details of the case titillated and shocked the public. Unlike the Winslow case, this one did not involve the traditionally respected public-school virtue, the honor of the small man fighting against the system for what is right—a chance to be heard—but, rather, the innocence, generosity, and truth of a woman whose private life was a public disgrace. In Rattigan's version the real contestants in the case are public versus private morality as much as they are the crown versus Alma Rattenbury and George Wood. They are also the antagonists in the private conflict within Mrs. Davenport, Tony's mother and head of the jury.

Alma Rattenbury, previously married twice, was the mother of two boys and the wife of an older man whom she affectionately called Ratz. He could not gratify her sexual needs but did provide her with a comfortable life-style, even though his stingy habits had forced Alma on occasion to lie. For example, to get money for a chauffeur's cap for George, she fabricated a story about needed engine repairs. Then, using a medical operation in London as an excuse, she extracted money from Ratz for an extravagant weekend in a London hotel with her young lover before her planned breaking of their liaison. Alma's sexual needs were filled by young men, and at the time of Ratz's murder they were being met by a boy-chauffeur, twenty years her junior, actually not much older than her elder son. When she and George returned from their London rendezvous, George, angered by a romantic episode between Alma and Ratz which he heard through locked doors, clubbed the old man to death.

Lurid as the details of this "Lady Chatterley" situation may seem, they were made even more revolting by disclosures that in themselves would have condemned her immediately in the eyes of the public and jury alike. She admitted, for example, that she and George would frequently enjoy sexual intercourse with her younger son asleep in the room, as it was the only circumstance in which they could remain undetected and, therefore, be free of hurting anyone. In both her financial and her sexual experiences Alma was forced to practice deceit and lying, an admission exploited by the prosecutor.

In order to save the other, each of the codefendants lied in his defense plea. George pleaded cocaine usage, and Alma used alcohol as her defense.

The real-life trial had a twist of legal genius, however, that even the most Scribean of well-made playwrights could hardly have devised. The device provided, both for the trial and its dramatized version, that climactic detail on which the outcome of the case hinged and on which the lives of the defendants depended. At the time of jury selection, defense counsel had approved Mrs. Davenport of Kensington as a member, even though she flatly stated at the time that she was prejudiced by newspaper accounts against Alma Rattenbury. Although the prosecution, sensing some potential usage of her bias by the defense later in the trial, warned against such usage, the latter in a brilliant coup injected that bias in clarifying in the jury's mind the differences between immorality and illegality.

To do so, defense counsel found it necessary to paint in vivid detail the times and places of sexual intercourse and the utter immorality of Alma. He seemed, indeed, to be influencing the jury against her. But, he continued, the fact that she was an immoral woman was not what she was on trial for. Did she or did she not kill Ratz? Then, having divulged the lies she told to protect George, the defense lawyer extracted from Alma her moral responsibility for the murder and, at the same time, her confession that the legal responsibility was not hers. She acquiesced to do so only after a visit at the jail from her son, whose compassion and understanding of her situation broke her resolve not to tell the truth.

Alma's lawyer repeatedly emphasized as did Alma that aberrational though her sexual behavior was, her one insistent principle was to enjoy life without hurting anyone. To do both, she had to resort to deceptions. In her actions and words she was always gentle, sensitive, generous, and loving.

The jury's deadlock was broken by the forewoman, Mrs. Davenport of Kensington, who persuaded the "guilty" votes to change. Alma was freed and George was convicted. Yet, a short time after the verdict Alma committed suicide and George's sentence was commuted. Her suicide occurred at the site at which she and George had made love. Stoner, the real George Wood, was still living at the time of Rattigan's play.

But the story of Alma is only half of Rattigan's drama. For he wove into the episodes of the Rattenbury trial the fictional narrative involving Mr. and Mrs. Davenport and their son, Tony, who was about the age of George. Mrs. Davenport is a veritable Aunt Edna of Kensington, whose husband, like Rattigan's father, Frank, had a life history of sexual affairs. Mrs. Davenport's typically British middle-class attitudes toward the immorality of Alma were only intensified by her own husband's aberrational sexual activity. Furthermore, her own son was experiencing his first sexual episode.

Tony's father, on a journey to the Continent with his son, had evaded making the necessary arrangements for a first sexual experience which Tony had desired. After discussing the matter with a friend, whose own experience was homosexual, Tony decided to take matters into his own hand and, as a result, became infected. Shamed by the consequence, he is even further embarrassed by the frequent and regular treatments he would have to administer to himself in his mother's bathroom. So he insists on leaving her to live with his father, who, although too embarrassed to be of much help, does understand and can eventually help him. The marital problem of the Davenports and that of their son only loosely tie in with the Rattenbury plot through the position of Mrs. Davenport as head of the trial jury.

In a thematic sense, however, the play is unified. The real-life Rattenbury story and the fictional Davenport narrative join in creating the archetypal Rattigan world. The Rattenburys lived in Bournemouth, the scene of *Separate Tables,* and the Davenports live at the moment in Kensington, for Rattigan, at least, the concentration of respectable, middle-class attitudes. Furthermore, Mrs. Davenport desires to buy a house in Bournemouth for herself and her son, but knows that she will have to forego the prospect if Alma is freed, for class attitudes in the person of her prospective seller would prohibit the sale to her. Yet Mrs. Davenport does vote honestly on the right issue, legality rather than morality, and so gives up both her biases for the moment and her Bournemouth prospect permanently.

Like Hester Collyer, she is alone at the end of the play, without husband, son, or Bournemouth residence. Upon hearing the news of Alma's suicide, she drunkenly shouts, "But I gave you life! . . . I gave you life! . . ." And in her most Kensingtonian voice, she adds, "And, might I say, at some considerable cost to my own? . . . Really, there's no justice. . . ."[11]

Repression, the *vice Anglais* with which Rattigan dealt in *In Praise of Love,* in this play takes the form of sexual inhibition and the unwillingness and inability of the Davenports of the Kensington world to discuss it. References by Mrs. Davenport and her sister to Alma as "that woman" abound; Tony and his homosexual friend refer to sex as "it." As the trial proceeds, Mrs. Davenport, the other members of the jury, and the newspaper-reading public are exposed to franker and freer language. Sexual intercourse is called just that. Beneath the hypocritical language facades gradually emerge the honesty and love that are Alma's real nature.

Alma Rattenbury belongs to that succession of Rattigan's heroines represented by Hester Collyer and Rose Fish who compulsively abandon conventionality for the love of a younger man. At one point in the trial, in response to the oft-reiterated point that it is the older woman who dominates the younger man, Alma protests, "Well I can only say that if anyone dominated anyone else, it was George who dominated me—"[12] Later Mrs. Davenport reflects upon the impact of Alma's words on her: "All the time, all the time that man was on at her: 'You were twenty years older, Madam. Twenty years older. I put it to you—you dominated that boy.' Do you know what she answered? 'When an older person loves a younger, it's the younger who dominates because the younger has so much more to give.' "[13]

Rattigan's own youthful homosexual liaisons involved older men and then, as he grew older, younger men. Domination by the young as well as their frequent unworthiness of love are recurrent themes that deepen in intensity and frankness in his later dramas. Here they exist explicitly. The older person gives materialistic largesse and in return receives emotional and sexual satisfaction. Alma gives enormous quantities of love to her husband; her children; her companion-friend, Irene Riggs; her lover; and even the wardens in jail. She compulsively requires the sexual love that only George can give her. Her capacity for love is so large that the one thing she cannot do is hurt anybody. Nothing in her life had ever shocked her mind, body, and spirit more than the discovery of her husband's body, battered to death by her lover. Her plea in her suicide note is, above every other, Rattigan's own: a plea for a beautiful world:

Eight o'clock. After so much running and walking I have got here. I should find myself just at this spot, where George and I once made love. It is beautiful here.

What a lovely world we are in, if only we would let ourselves see it. It must be easier to be hanged than to have to do the job oneself. But that's just my bad luck. Pray God nothing stops me. God bless my children and look after them. One has to be bold to do this thing. But it is beautiful here, and I am alone. Thank God for peace at last.[14]

The coroner's report read that Alma Rattenbury had been seen in a meadow by a laborer, "a lady sitting and writing." However, "when he reached her she was dead, her head lying in one foot of water."[15] Among other "random thoughts scribbled in pencil on the backs of envelopes" was one: "I want to make it perfectly clear that no one is responsible for my action. I made up my mind during the trial that if George was sentenced to death I would not survive him—"[16] Alma could not live with the thought of having injured anyone. Had Rattigan provided the ending for her story, he may have chosen a fate similar to Hester Collyer's or Rose Fish's, but in this story life outdid art.

Structurally, *Cause Célèbre* continues Rattigan's style of the dual plot. The two plots constitute a modern-day morality play in which good and evil in the shape of public morality and private truth do battle with each other, Mrs. Davenport in not allowing bias to cloud her judgment and Alma Rattenbury in insisting on moral responsibility for the events. Scenes in the play alternate between the two plots, one reinforcing the other thematically as Mrs. Davenport moves toward her decision. Critics generally had reservations about the effectiveness of the two plots. To this writer, they do work.

Like *A Bequest to the Nation,* which was first a television drama, *Cause Célèbre* was written for radio, accounting in part for a fluidity that may be difficult to achieve on the stage. There are flashbacks, for instance, of Alma's last scene with Ratz in their bedroom and of her final wandering in the meadow before her suicide. Stage lighting and dimming could accomplish the fluidity, but less forcefully than the imagination can in the hearing or reading of the play.

Much has been written in the press of Rattigan's getting up from his sickbed to attend the London opening in July 1977. With the knowledge of his own imminent death, the real-life comments of Alma about the beauty of life and God's intention that it be enjoyed must have been moving for Rattigan, the cast, and the audience. There were no heroics or sentimentality in his last play—as there were not for the most part, in his other plays. Sentiment—yes, much of it. And the small heroisms of the average man and of failed men, yes. Even more importantly there was entertainment which brought both laughter and tears by means of well-told stories. His life and art, all told, ended with the final curtain of *Cause Célèbre*, foreboding his own death a few months later. It ended with neither the Eliotic bang nor whimper but with the mellowed and firm belief in the life-loving Alma Rattenburys and the slowly changing Mrs. Davenports. Finally, his early Harrovian dream in which he was wildly excited by the line "The curtain rises to disclose," which had been coming true for him for so many years, was completely realized with the final curtain of *Cause Célèbre*.

Chapter Fourteen

A Summing Up

"I don't write Terence Rattigan plays but I think I have more in common with Rattigan than with Robert Wilson. We attempt to be coherent tellers of tales."[1] This statement by Tom Stoppard, made two years after the opening of Rattigan's last play, may seem surprising to those familiar with *Rosencrantz and Guildenstern Are Dead, Travesties, Jumpers, Every Good Boy Deserves Favour,* and other plays by a prolific playwright of the post-1956 dramatic era. For his play about the two minor characters from *Hamlet* established Stoppard almost immediately as one of the new, experimental, perhaps absurdist, dramatists on the English stage. Particularly noted in the reviews of his plays were the brilliant displays of language fireworks, superbly rendered by actors such as John Wood and Michael Hordern. Audiences reacted with some puzzlement to his enigmatic situations, as they did to those in the plays of Harold Pinter. More recently, however, the fireworks have diminished, and the storytelling Stoppard is in stronger evidence, as in *Night and Day.* The narrative tradition of which Stoppard speaks is that of Terence Rattigan, and for all their difference in language usage, Stoppard has spoken in admiring terms of Terence Rattigan, as though to underscore this bond.

Action as Narrative Art

Rattigan's plays are characterized by narrative techniques of the ancient balladeer, whose action begins immediately with the opening lines. This is not the technique of the Scribean well-made play or the well-made problem play of Ibsen, Pinero, or Galsworthy, whose first acts are heavy with exposition and whose play action does not begin in some cases until the end of a long first act or the beginning of the second. Ronnie Winslow's unannounced, stealthy return home after his dismissal from Osborne Naval Academy opens *The Winslow Boy,* and the events involving an entire family and, indeed a whole nation, build immediately from that initial event. Belabored psychological, sociological, or political details from the past have no place here, and it is the straightforwardness of the ancient balladeer's tale which gains and holds audience interest.

This immediacy is nowhere so pronounced as in another stealthy action of a young student, Taplow in *The Browning Version,* who enters his classics master's home for a tutorial, helps himself to two pieces of chocolate, and then furtively replaces one. The action continues unremittingly in events that fall on the schoolmaster until they break his emotional rigidities. Schoolboys George Matcham and Tony Davenport very early in *A Bequest to the Nation* and *Cause Célèbre* similarly begin the action in those plays.

Labored exposition of the conventional playwright, frequently in the persons of servants and minor characters, is not the technique of Rattigan. Rather, action itself propels the characters into emotional states long suppressed.

Emotional Climaxes

Consequently, the point of highest tension, the climax, is not one of event as in the tradition of the formula play, but one of emotional truth realized by the character in a moment when that emotion can no longer be suppressed or when that truth questions the values that have caused the suppression. In some plays like *The Browning Version* the questioning has already occurred over a long period of time, and it remains merely to break through the surfaces of the routine events in the master's final days at the school. Events lead immediately from the opening incident to the climax in which he breaks down emotionally in a gripping scene. Thus, narrative action serves as Rattigan's primary means of character revelation.

In the history plays, particularly, the moment of truth consists of the climactic questions to which the narrative leads, such as "Where did it all go wrong?" in *Adventure Story.* In the last three plays Rattigan's climaxes consist of both emotion and questioning, creating a more complex texture missing in the earlier plays and sacrificing some of the dramatic effect. In *Separate Tables* Rattigan strikes a balance between the two unequaled in any of his other plays. The delicately woven conflict between personal desires and social tolerance is resolved by events which lead inevitably to Sibyl's climactic defiance of her mother and the Major's acceptance by the hotel's occupants, both supremely understated moments of truth. The delicacy of the climax here contrasts sharply with the histrionics of *A Bequest to the Nation,* similar to the difference in styles between the poetry of *The Glass*

Menagerie and the high theatricality of *A Streetcar Named Desire* by Tennessee Williams.

Without the delicacy of *Separate Tables* or the artistic histrionics of *A Bequest to the Nation,* the climax in *In Praise of Love* seems expected and loses some punch. Lydia and Sebastian Cruttwell, equally strong individuals, battle their respective ways to an accommodation of their inequalities. Lydia's physical blows to Sebastian seem healthy, normal reactions and far more deserved and kindly than those inflicted on each other by John Malcolm and Ann Shankland or the verbal blows Millie deals to Crocker-Harris or those society has inflicted on Sibyl Railton-Bell and the Major.

Most poetically handled of all Rattigan's climaxes is that in *Cause Célèbre* in Alma's decision to tell the truth at the trial, the turning point of both the trial and her life. The compulsions of conscience and emotion fuse in a totally satisfying whole, defused of sentimentality and melodrama by Mrs. Davenport's sense of futility upon learning of Alma's suicide. Rattigan's climax, here provided by real life, is not mechanically contrived but has the emotional authenticity of art at its best. An important feature of his narrative art, these high moments round out the techniques by which he shapes his characters.

Natural Endings

Equally important in his narrative style are the natural endings of Rattigan's dramas that contrast sharply with the contrived conclusions of the well-made play. His final scenes follow the curvatures of life in the tradition of Chekhov. In both writers, life continues with some few changes caused by the events and outside forces during the course of the narrative. Changes occur mostly as externalizations of long-repressed emotion or of questions which have slowly developed over a lifetime.

Full grown in adults, these questions and emotional confusion are incipient in the many schoolboys and young adults of Rattigan's dramas. Whatever the stage or nature of the problems, life goes on. Schoolboys return to school; the younger adults continue, like Joey Cruttwell, who will survive his mother's death and somehow effect a reconciliation of sorts with his father and who will continue writing; older adults, even when emotionally or sexually frustrated, indeed crippled—such as the Shanklands, the Railton-Bells and Major Pollock, Hester Collyer, Andrew Crocker-Harris, Rose Fish, Lady Hamilton and Lady Nelson, Sebastian

Cruttwell, and the Davenport family—continue with what remains to them in life, in full awareness of what life holds for them. All have exercised their obligations to themselves with honesty and dignity. All have found or regained, however painfully, some link to the human community. Some, as in the case of Major Pollock, Andrew Crocker-Harris, and Alma Rattenbury, have heightened the consciousness and conscience of an intolerantly conventional society. In his narrative style, Rattigan serves as a social critic and a conscience for his times as do the post-1956 dramatists in more fashionable sociological and psychological ways. His is a narrative and emotional appeal to a broad spectrum of theater audiences.

Rattigan's Chekhovian sense of the continuity of things can be seen particularly in the strong yet deliberately mundane and flat statements made by characters at the conclusions of the plays. These statements are a call to a resumption of life, such as Andrew Crocker-Harris's quiet "We mustn't let our dinner get cold" or Sebastian's telling Joey, "Go on. Move, Joey" when underneath the routine of the chess game lies the agonizing knowledge of Lydia's impending death. By narrative means, Rattigan's subtextual meanings, like Chekhov's so-called plotless plays, reveal states of being in which internal changes have long since occurred. Characters may be bored, troubled, life-damaged, isolated from communication with others, and alienated from their times, but they do continue to survive and to find some degree of community and communication. Most of all, they are aware in an existential sense of their condition. From self-knowledge they gather what strength they can, and they endure. Affirmation of life is there in the most flawed and vulnerable characters. The Sibyl Railton-Bells of Rattigan, like the Laura Wingfields of Tennessee Williams, may be denied emotional health, but like the characters of Chekhov they are not totally alienated from life. Their deliberately banal statements, usually found near the end of the play, express Rattigan's insistence on the conquering of hope and, therefore, despair.

In this respect, for all his much-talked-about romanticism, Rattigan seems more closely allied to experiential existentialism. Although his realistic narrative techniques may have little in common with the sur-realistic stories of Beckett or Pinter, the angst of his characters, who are drawn on the scale of the average man, evokes the experiences that Beckett has dramatized philosophically and Pinter psychologically. Rattigan's emphasis is emotional. Maintaining his natural resistance to the experi-ments in surrealism and absurdism, which by the time of his death had themselves settled into a convention, Rattigan dramatized naturalistically the emotions of an age stretching from 1933 to 1977, during which theatrical and political wars changed stage conventions and social patterns.

So, in spite of the well-made-play label, with its pejorative association of emptiness that has been too glibly applied to them, Rattigan's dramas resist that categorization.

Periodization

Periodization is equally difficult, for he alternated light comedies with serious plays, farces with war dramas, domestic problem plays with history plays, romances with courtroom dramas. One decade which can be singularly characterized, however, is that of the 1950s, before and after the Osborne revolution. Before 1956, *The Deep Blue Sea* and *Separate Tables* solidly established him as an important serious dramatist, and after 1956, *Variation on a Theme, Ross,* and *Man and Boy* continued his intense dramatic portraits of vulnerable human beings. When, after his seven-year absence, Rattigan returned to the stage in 1970, he resumed his writing in this genre. Labeled by some as the artist of humiliation, he continued his dramatic portrayal of flawed characters. Although the dramas lost some of the sharp edge and focus of earlier works, they became more complex and more richly textured.

In a more conventional four-part grouping, Rattigan's plays fall into four periods, the basis for their arrangement in *The Collected Plays of Terence Rattigan.* Volume 1 contains the early dramas from *First Episode* (1933) to *The Winslow Boy* (1946). Thematic and stylistic characteristics of this early group of plays deepen in the next period in plays from *The Browning Version* (1948) to *The Deep Blue Sea* (1952) of Volume 2. In the 1950s these concerns reach their consummate dramatization in *Separate Tables,* but they exist forcefully in the other dramas of the decade (Vol. 3). Finally, from *Man and Boy* (1963) through *Cause Célèbre* (1977), Rattigan's pervasive themes—emotional repression, the pain of emotional inequalities, the conflict of fathers and sons—achieve their fullest and most outspoken expression.

If labels, categories, and periodizations of Rattigan's plays present problems, his thematic concerns do not. At the heart of his narratives are the relationships between parents and sons or between marital partners, whose inequalities of age, social status, or sexual-emotional needs create conflicts within the individual and between him and his society.

Themes: Fathers and Sons

The first of these appears as a lesser motif in a play as early as *French Without Tears*, in Alan's decision to become a writer rather than a diplomat, as his father wished. In *Love in Idleness* a young son returns from Canada to face a situation of a mother living with her lover. Then there is Ronnie in *The Winslow Boy*, too young for the problems of the adult world in matters of career or romance, but symbolic of the cherished English right to be heard, no matter how small a person may be. Close on his heels in Rattigan's gallery of youthful characters is Taplow, the student who learns that even the "Himmler of the lower fifth" deserves understanding and sympathy. Relations between man and boy are more adult in *Who Is Sylvia?* as the son tries to understand his father and even proffer advice on his career. The father-son theme becomes central in a number of succeeding plays, such as *The Final Test*, in which the plot turns on the son's refusal to attend his father's test match in favor of visiting a poet whom he admires. In *Man and Boy* the complexly plotted narrative seems almost consumed by the hate-love feelings between father and illegitimate son—this time the interests of the business world and musical aspirations of the son collide—that reach their most intense expression in what can be seen as a modern morality play.

Finally, in the last three plays, as discussed in preceding chapters, the father-son conflict is dealt with as a rite of initiation into adulthood between young George Matcham and his famous Uncle Horatio, between Joey and Sebastian Cruttwell, and between Tony Davenport and his parents, who have refused to help him in his plea for information about and understanding of his sexual problems. Indeed, even in *Separate Tables*, the crippled Sibyl and Major are the direct result of conventional, dishonest parental attitudes toward sex. One can see in the succession of play after play Rattigan's increasing concern in developing the parent–child relationship until it reaches its frankest expression in his last play.

Themes: Inequalities of Relationships

The second of Rattigan's familial themes is that of the inequalities of domestic and romantic liaisons. Frequently, as in the case of Hester Collyer, the successful husband can give her everything except what she needs most, the passion that only Freddie, her social inferior, can provide. However, her lover cannot give her the steadiness of attention, love, and financial and moral support which her husband stands ready to offer for the

taking. In the experience of women characters such as Hester, Rose, and
Alma, the men who satisfy emotional and sexual needs are weak, so it is
the young or the socially inferior who are the powerful figures in a
relationship and who dominate the older and the conventionally stronger
person. In Rattigan's first produced play, the young Tony Wodehouse
dominates the older actress, who knows that she will suffer for a long time,
whereas Tony will go on easily to his next love. In Rattigan's last play,
inequalities abound. Alma dominates her older husband; she in turn is
dominated by her younger lover, and even her young son is the reason she
makes the most crucial decision to tell the truth.

To reinforce the theme of inequalities and repressions, Rattigan used the
fictional jurywoman Mrs. Davenport as a framework for his characterization of Alma. Mrs. Davenport herself is having marital problems, and her
young son's first sexual experiences complicate those problems and bear
directly on her decisions regarding the trial. At one point she refers to an
older woman on the Continent who had shown interest in their young son,
causing her to spirit Tony back to England as quickly as possible. The
sexual intimacies involved in the Rattenbury case are indeed close to her
domestic situation. She becomes in Rattigan's thickening of the texture of
the play a symbol of his Aunt Edna of Kensington, with her middle-class
distaste for and repression of honesty about sexual matters. The consequence is a rigid inability to discuss these matters with her son. In spite of
his good intentions, Tony's father is equally unable to help him. Mrs.
Davenport and Alma Rattenbury illustrate negative and positive influences on the young. They illuminate Rattigan's concern with marital and
sibling problems, and, particularly, his sharp focus on the influence of the
younger, weaker, and unconventional on the older, stronger, and conventional person.

The inequality theme reaches its most tempestuous form, however, in
the romantic triangle of Horatio Nelson, Emma Hamilton, and Frances
Nelson, and here the domestic drama reaches into national emotions and
eventually into a matter of life and death for the hero. All three are so bent
in their needs and desires that they are powerless to change. Lady Nelson is
everything that society would approve in the wife of the national hero, and
Lady Hamilton's coarseness is the antithesis of that approved life-style.
The conflict in Lord Nelson between his overwhelming personal needs and
the demands social approval make on him can be resolved only in the
real-life manner: his death in battle. For the women there is no resolution
but to continue living in their respective ways. The characters in actual life
seem so much larger than life that, performed insensitively, they could

indeed become caricatures. Romantic and marital inequalities in this trio of characters have no resolution and allow no accommodation of each other. But Rattigan's most civilized, yet perhaps most cruel, mismatch is reserved for Lydia and Sebastian Cruttwell. A central-eastern European refugee from Hitler and the Russians, Lydia is as unlike the undemonstrative Sebastian as a wife can be. But both are intelligently sensitive and work their way through their deceptions and disguises with finesse and dignity, with their repressed emotions exploding at last in Lydia's striking of her husband. The pent-up feeling of years, although healthier because Lydia is Sebastian's equal in strength, is similar to Crocker-Harris's emotional breakdown and even to that one brief, flickering emotion between Antonescu and his son. All are affirmations of humanness, humanity long repressed. Emotional inequalities are reconciled in the recognition by all three—mother, father, son—of their deepest-seated compatibility expressed in the father-son resumption of the chess game as Lydia, terminally ill, leaves the room.

Even in lighter plays such as *While the Sun Shines* mismatches form the fabric of the comedy. Elizabeth, who will marry Lord Harpenden, experiences the "white-hot passion" explained to her by the French officer when she becomes intoxicated in the company of the American serviceman. Her sensible marriage to Harpenden excludes such satisfaction. Patricia in *Flare Path* similarly makes a choice which would exclude the romance she would have experienced with Peter. The situations of the early plays and the comedies, in particular, contain the seeds of the disillusion that pervades the characters in the serious dramatic portraits that began in the 1940s with Andrew Crocker-Harris and that gathered momentum in the next three decades of Rattigan's career.

Themes: Existential Choice-Making

Inextricably involved in the two themes just discussed is a third that becomes increasingly evident with every play. It is that of the existential choices his characters make, existential experientially rather than philosophically. They know only too well the consequences of their choices. They know that the choice is between a driving personal need for fulfillment and the conventional expectations of those nearest them or of society. The need frequently takes the form of giving love to someone who is unworthy of it or who rejects it. Rose Fish wants to give love to a daughter who does not want it. Her previous husbands did not need the type of love she needs to give, so she chooses the much younger ballet dancer, Ron, over the tycoon, Kurt Mast, who wants to marry her. In fact, her choice of Ron includes the probability of imminent death, as she will not be going to the healthful climate prescribed by her physician.

Alma Rattenbury can give wifely affection to her much older husband and motherly love to her children, but she needs to fulfill her sexual passion in young George Wood, in the face of social respectability. Like Rose Fish in the earlier play, she has a female companion also, upon whom she can bestow some of the abundance of feeling she must give. But it is the much younger man who is needed by both women to receive their love and to dominate. For Alma, George's domination becomes a stranglehold which eventually results in George's murder of her husband.

In 1942 in *Flare Path* the choice made by Patricia is determined to some extent by the patriotic tempo of the times. But in 1952 in *The Deep Blue Sea* Hester's choice in leaving her husband for Freddie is not affected by outside events. The inequalities in the latter are not absorbed in a common cause and become so much more painful. The choice becomes at the same time clearer and more compelling. Choice for Rattigan's characters is indication of emotional identity, without which metamorphosis into living corpses such as Crocker-Harris and, even more so, Gregor Antonescu, is inevitable. Both of these characters were trapped by their own early choices in identities that hardened to their own emotional needs in later years. One character in Rattigan's dramas who did not allow himself to become a corpse emotionally is Lord Nelson. For the needs of the night, he risked the daytime respect of a whole nation as he continuously chose his coarse mistress over his refined wife.

In earlier characters either the social situation or injured psyches precluded the possibility of happiness. Yet even their small triumphs were more than enough for the failures and humiliations they had borne, from Catherine Winslow right on through Alma Rattenbury. But Alma Rattenbury is Rattigan's fullest expression of the matter of choice, for she considers her inner morality more important than that imposed by society. Above everything else she considered love and, consequently, the need *not* to hurt as the very principle of life itself. Her choices were made exclusively out of her need to give love. As she exercises her will freely, she gives seemingly inexhaustible stores of love to husband, companion, lover, and children. Society is shocked at her behavior, yet she has injured no one. The injury perpetrated by socially approved attitudes, however, is enormous, as they force her to practice deceptions.

It was Strindberg who so tempestuously dramatized the mother-wife-mistress needs of his male characters. In a curious turn of the same experience, Rattigan deals with the mother-wife-lover needs of his female characters in a male-oriented society. Their needs change and dictate their choices. Made in time, the choices can provide fulfillment. Made too late or not tolerated by existing social structure, they can be devastating. Nevertheless, choice by its very existence, apart from its consequences, is a sign of life. From its very tenuous nature in Hester Collyer to its poetic vitality in Alma Rattenbury, from its healthy state in Patricia Graham or Catherine Winslow to its emotionally diseased state in Lydia Cruttwell, it must be made and its consequences endured. And it must be made out of basic human needs, very often the need to give love. Like Madame Ranevskaya of Chekhov's *The Cherry Orchard,* Rattigan's characters have emotions whose expression external conditions thwart. Unconventional choices free these emotions in varying degrees and frequently at great cost.

The matter of choice operates also in Rattigan's parent-child theme. The son's defiance of a parent's choice of career runs through many variations from *French Without Tears* on through the hostility between father and son in *The Final Test, Man and Boy,* and *In Praise of Love.* Even in comic romances such as *Love in Idleness* and *Who Is Sylvia?* a son influences a mother in a decision regarding her lover or he advises and chides an errant father.

But it is in Rattigan's last three plays that the integrity of the boy seems to challenge the deceit, hypocrisy, or inhumanity of the man, and the challenge remains intact in the face of disillusioning realities.

George Matcham, against the wishes of the entire Nelson family, chooses to deliver Lady Nelson's letter to the Admiral. Joey Cruttwell, also disillusioned by the treatment of one parent by the other, experiences hurt as a result of his father's insensitivity to his first television play. His choices in regard to his feelings about his father must await the death of his terminally ill mother, but she has in her last days already begun to influence him. Christopher Rattenbury, George Wood, and Tony Davenport are in respectively increasing positions of choice-making, but it is Tony Davenport who is Rattigan's final comment on the parent-child relationship that forces the boy to learn adult realities, alone and ignorant. For in Tony, Rattigan fictionalizes his own experience. Shocking as the story of Alma Rattenbury and George Wood seemed to the English public in 1935, even more shocking is the devastation wrought on the young Tony by the convention-ridden inability of parents to advise him on sexual matters when he pleads for that help. The only choice left Tony is no choice at all. He must discover for himself the realities about which his parents were unable to advise him. Even his peer, Randolph Brown, more interested in homosexuality, was of no help. Finally, after the humiliation of his having contracted venereal disease from a prostitute, Tony chooses to leave his mother, with whom he has been living.

In earlier plays, the matter of choice involving the young and their relations with the adult world, especially with fathers and surrogate fathers, was simpler. Ronnie Winslow is tempted to change the letter of dismissal when he first arrives from Osborne. He chooses not to. Young Taplow of the fifth-form classics class chooses to return one of two stolen chocolates to the box in the schoolmaster's house. His involvement in the adult world of choice-making is complicated when he feels something for the schoolmaster even though his classmates deride Crocker-Harris as the Himmler of the lower fifth. Further his choice of the Browning version of *Agamemnon* as a farewell gift externalizes his instinctive sympathy for the dull classics master. Unknown to Taplow, his choice becomes the means for the one expression of emotion the master has allowed himself in many years, and, in consequnce, for the master's verbalization of the inequality, now an unbridgeable gap, between him and his wife. The freedom the master gained from his verbalization then allows him to declare his independence from Millie and to choose the speaking order at commencement activities. Boy provided man in this case with the momentary fulfillment of an emotional need necessary even to survive.

So for the adults in Rattigan's dramatic world choice meant survival; for the many schoolboys choices are the means by which boy enters manhood. For the latter the rites of passage involve the inevitable loss of innocence, and for the former an increasingly painful angst. Personal ideals are soberingly challenged by the realities of the outside world, but the integrity of man or boy holds fast by means of choice. Rattigan is both romantic and existentialist at the same time.

Themes: The "Vice-Anglais": Emotional Repression

Forming the bond among all the themes in Rattigan's dramas is what is referred to in *In Praise of Love* as the "vice Anglais," the inability to express emotion which may go so far as to become the absence of it altogether. The metamorphosis has already taken its toll on characters such as Crocker-Harris by the time of the initial action of the play. Existing in varying degrees in most plays, this transformation of man into corpse achieves its ultimate evil form in Gregor Antonescu. It is a *fait accompli* at the play's beginning. The course of the metamorphosis, however, is most explicitly dramatized in *In Praise of Love* as a damagingly repressive habit ingrained in the very system and character of the British. Its tentacles reach out into all relationships, squeezing the life from some and crippling in varying degrees the lives of others. The lies and deceptions into which people are forced become a habit which eventually becomes a substitute for emotional expression. A symbol of British wit and civility, Sebastian Cruttwell hides his real feelings in the cruel games he plays, for they become the only means by which he can control emotions. The control becomes his vulnerability, and the games become lies. Game-playing becomes his only means of communication with his wife and his son. And this means is not sufficient—in fact, it is destructive—where important matters of career or of death are at stake. So the distance between him and his family becomes unbridgeable until the moment in the play that Lydia deals him a physical blow.

Sebastian Cruttwell's games are not too different from those Osborne's Jimmy Porter plays in *Look Back in Anger*. Nor are they very different from the enigmatic actions in the plays of Harold Pinter or David Storey, in which characters play games in order to keep from knowing and being known. Being known is a vulnerability to be avoided at all costs. In Peter Nichols's *A Day in the Death of Joe Egg* the parents of a mongoloid child can tolerate their misfortune only by playing games, and in *The National Health* the terminally ill, as well as the hospital staff, make continual games of life. Games and role-playing are the channels for emotional expression. In Rattigan's dramas, corpses can result from such expression.

In earlier dramatists such as George Bernard Shaw, emotions are channeled into witty word games. In Galsworthy's *Justice,* the frequently referred to precursor of Rattigan's *The Winslow Boy,* the emotion is heavy with the weight of social criticism, and a sentimentalized melodrama ensues. Rattigan's dramatizing of emotional needs of people avoids the extremes of sentimentality on the one hand or of the total absence of emotional expression on the other. His characters attempt to deal in a very private way with their emotional needs even when they run into the stone wall of a tradition that frowns on demonstrative conduct. The British inhibition is particularly pronounced in sexual matters, so that "tasteful" control of emotion easily metamorphoses into lack of emotion.

Repression of emotion creates a dis-ease between partners in a marriage and between parents and children, but most destructively it results in social hypocrisy such as that represented by the residents of the Beauregard Hotel in Bournemouth or the Davenports of Kensington.

Although Rattigan is neither the first nor last writer to focus on emotional dishonesty and social hypocrisy so strongly, he has taken it from the arena of social criticism to that of private need. His personalization of the problem creates strength even in his weakest characters and inner success in his most failed and flawed people. Consequently, they are not victims to be pitied but living beings to be sympathized with and admired.

Thematic Discourses

He captures these major themes frequently in brief monologues by certain of his major characters. Most of these have already been pointed out in the discussion of the plays in which they appear. There is the advice of the defrocked doctor, Mr. Miller, to Hester Collyer about going beyond hope and, therefore, beyond despair, an existentialist choice repeated in word and action by many other characters. As early as 1939 in *After the Dance* this mood permeates the characters of that pre–World War II drama. Another important disquisition on the nature of marital love and its inequalities which preclude emotional fulfillment is Crocker-Harris's analysis of his and Millie's twenty-year empty marriage. More explicitly than any other character in Rattigan's dramatic tales, Lord Nelson, with the freedom that only a self-assured person can exercise, explains the irresistibility of the nighttime needs that more than compensate for the daytime embarrassments caused by his very unconventional mistress. Finally, there is the powerful poetic discourse by Alma Rattenbury on the necessity to give love and on the power of the receiver over the giver or the younger over the older. In all of Rattigan's work Alma's poignancy is surpassed only by that of Major Pollock in the inarticulately poetic confession he makes to Sibyl Railton-Bell. It is in these monologues that the implicit truths underlying the dialogue and narrative action find articulation and focus.

Oblique and Delicate Playwright

Making no claims to revolutionizing techniques of playwriting or to psychological, sociological, or philosophical profundities, Rattigan's plays encompass in their modest fashion fifty years of mid-twentieth-century stage history in both England and America. They are characterized by a refinement of mind and style that time is already beginning to prove are more than English public-school virtues and sleek techniques, as his strongest attackers claimed. Kenneth Tynan's labeling of him as the Formosa of the British theater and then Rattigan's subsequent creation of Aunt Edna, as well as his self-instituted debate in a "battle of the theatres," hounded him throughout most of his career. Yet, in what Hilary Spurling described as that "tricky but crucial (and so far almost wholly neglected) stretch of contemporary theatrical history when the stage became society's distorting mirror," Rattigan occupies a prominent place as the "oblique and delicate playwright of inarticulacy, repression, self-punishment, above all the damage people do to themselves."[2]

Yet this genre tells only half of Rattigan's story. For up to 1953, when *The Sleeping Prince* was produced, he wrote a long string of comedies and farces in which he proved himself to be as delicate in articulating the health and vibrancy of his characters as he was in the portrayal of the highly vulnerable people of his later plays. One type of character and play reflects the maturation of the other. The succession of comedies by the mellowed, bittersweet romances of the last plays matches the traditional progress of the English playwrights of the past. Rattigan is an important dramatist in that tradition.

Each of his dramas is a progressive refinement of that sense of theater of which he spoke so frequently, a sense which insisted on the duality of the playwright as both writer and audience. The loss of touch with the audience which characterized the dramatic experimentation in the revolutionary stage events since 1956 was caused to a certain degree by the elitism of many of the changes. Rattigan never lost touch. To move an audience to laughter and to tears, rather than to confusion or puzzlement, was always his primary goal, and he consistently maintained sight of that goal. Of his contemporary dramatists, he alone survived the upheavals of the 1950s with his traditionalist approach which renewed itself in his stage comeback of 1970. And before the experimental waves subsided into the mainstream of theater history, Rattigan once more became a part of that stream. His comedies, history plays, and moving dramas about flawed or failed characters course their way unerringly down the moral and emotional mainstream of their troubled times.

Notes and References

Preface

1. Harold Hobson, "The Playwright Who Always Hid His Pain," *Sunday Times,* 4 December 1977, p. 35.
2. Bernard Drew, interview with Tom Stoppard, "Lifestyles," Westchester-Rockland Newspapers, 20 January 1977.

Chapter One

1. *National Union Catalog,* Pre-1956 Imprints, p. 149.
2. Kenneth Tynan, "Jackpot Rattigan," *Evening Standard,* 1 July 1953.
3. Ibid.
4. Terence Rattigan, Preface to *Collected Plays* (London, 1953), 2:xv. Subsequent references to the *Collected Plays* are indicated by volume and page numbers.
5. 2:viii.
6. Ibid.
7. Ibid.
8. 2:xiv, xv.
9. John Simon, "Rattigan Talks to John Simon," *Theatre Arts* 46 (April 1962):24.
10. Bryan Forbes, *Dame Edith Evans* (Boston: Little, Brown, 1977), p. 148.
11. Philip Oakes, "Living for the Present," *Times,* 1 February 1976, p. 35.
12. 1:xiv.
13. Ibid.
14. Oakes, "Living for the Present," p. 35.
15. Simon, "Rattigan Talks," p. 24.
16. Tynan, "Jackpot Rattigan."
17. Oakes, "Living for the Present," p. 35.
18. Sheridan Morley, "Terence Rattigan at 65," *Times,* 9 May 1977.
19. Ibid.
20. Oakes, "Living for the Present," p. 35.
21. Anthony Curtis, "Professional Man and Boy," *Plays and Players* 25, no. 5 (February 1978):23.
22. Ibid.

23. Ibid.
24. Ibid., p. 22.
25. Ibid.

Chapter Two

1. 1:xx.
2. 2:ix.
3. 2:x.
4. 2:xi.
5. 2:xv.
6. Barry Hyams, "A Chat with Terence Rattigan," *Theatre Arts* 40 (November 1956):23.
7. 1:xviii, xix.
8. 1:xix.
9. Ibid.
10. 1:xix, xx.
11. 2:48.
12. 2:365.
13. 2:366.
14. 1:xx, xxi.
15. Hyams, "A Chat," p. 22.
16. 2:xix.
17. Hyams, "A Chat," p. 20.

Chapter Three

1. John Barber, *Daily Telegraph,* 1 December 1977. Obituary.
2. 1:xix.
3. Peter Ustinov, *Dear Me* (Boston, 1977), p. 338.
4. John Russell Taylor, *The Rise and Fall of the Well Made Play* (New York, 1967), p. 144.
5. Barry Hyams, "A Chat," p. 22.
6. 3:xxvii.
7. Ibid.
8. 3:xxiv.
9. 3:xxv.
10. 3:xvii.
11. Ibid.
12. 3:viii, ix.
13. Richard Gilman, "Out Goes Absurdism—In Comes the New Naturalism," *New York Times,* 19 March 1978, sec. 2, p. 1.
14. Stephen Stanton, ed., *Camille and Other Plays* (New York: Hill and Wang, 1957), p. xii, xiii.

15. Ibid., p. xix.
16. Harold Hobson, "The Playwright," p. 35.
17. Ibid.
18. Robert Muller, "Soul-Searching with Terence Rattigan," *Daily Mail*, 30 April 1960.
19. Cecil Beaton, *Memoirs of the 40's* (New York, 1972), p. 101.
20. Ibid.
21. Hyams, "A Chat," p. 22.
22. John Barber, "Rattigan's Return," *Daily Telegraph*, 30 July 1973.
23. Alan Brien, "London Lights Are All Aglow," *Theatre Arts* 45 (February 1961):59.
24. Taylor, *Rise and Fall*, p. 165.

Chapter Four

1. 1:vii.
2. *New York Times*, 13 September 1934, p. 18, col. 1.
3. *Times*, 27 January 1934, p. 8, col. c.
4. Terence Rattigan, *First Episode*, manuscript, Act II, p. 14.
5. *Times*, 27 January 1934, p. 8, col. c.
6. Rattigan, *First Episode*, Act I, p. 51.
7. Muller, "Soul-Searching."
8. Ronald Hayman, "Life for Father," *Times*, 19 September 1970, p. 19.
9. *Times*, 17 January 1940, p. 6, col. d.
10. Ibid.
11. *New Statesman*, 27 January 1940.
12. Terence Rattigan, *After the Dance*, from *Six Plays of 1939* (London, 1939), p. 34.
13. *Times*, 22 June 1939, p. 14, col. b.
14. Rattigan, *After the Dance*, p. 66.
15. Geoffrey Matthews, "The Winsome Boy of Sixty," *Evening News*, 10 June 1971.
16. *New York Times*, 16 July 1939, sec. IX, p. 2, col. 1.
17. *New Statesman*, 1 July 1939, p. 14.
18. *New York Times*, 16 July 1939, sec. IX, p. 2, col. 1.

Chapter Five

1. Morley, "Rattigan at 65."
2. Taylor, *Rise and Fall*, p. 148.
3. Morley, "Rattigan at 65."
4. *New York Times*, 19 March 1974, p. 28, col. 1.
5. 1:82.
6. 1:64.

7. 1:69.
8. *New York Times,* 19 March 1974, p. 28, col. 1.
9. William Douglas Home, "Terence Rattigan Remembered," *Times,* 10 February 1978.
10. Ibid.
11. Ibid.
12. Ibid.
13. 1:xx.
14. Ibid.
15. Ibid.

Chapter Six

1. 1:xiv.
2. Ibid.
3. Roger Marvell, *"Flare Path,"* *New Statesman and Nation,* 22 August 1942, p. 124.
4. Ibid.
5. Lewis Nichols, *"Flare Path,"* *New York Times,* 24 December 1942, p. 20, col. 2.
6. W. A. Darlington, review of *Flare Path* in *New York Times,* 23 August 1942, sec. VIII, p. 1, col. 6.
7. 1:152.
8. Ibid.
9. 1:150.
10. 1:200.
11. Taylor, *Rise and Fall,* p. 150.
12. 1:228.
13. Muller, "Soul-Searching."
14. *Times,* 28 December 1943, p. 6, col. b.
15. Ibid.
16. Lewis Nichols, *"While the Sun Shines,"* *New York Times,* 20 September 1944, p. 21, col. 3.
17. Ibid.
18. 2:xviii.
19. *New Statesman and Nation,* 30 December 1944.
20. *New York Times,* 7 January 1945, sec. 11, p. 2, col. 3.
21. Rosamund Gilder, "Sprightly Entertainment," *Theatre Arts* 30 (March 1946):133.
22. *New York Times,* 1 September 1946, sec. 11, p. 1, col. 1.
23. Ibid.
24. Ibid.
25. 1:325.
26. Louis Calta, Rattigan's obituary, *New York Times,* 1 December 1977.

Chapter Seven

1. 1:xvii.

Chapter Eight

1. Michael Darlow and Gillian Hodson, *Terence Rattigan: The Man and His Work* (London, 1979), p. 35.
2. 2:5.
3. 2:7, 8.
4. 2:9.
5. 2:31–32.
6. 2:20.
7. Ibid.
8. 2:35, 36.
9. 2:37.
10. 2:38.
11. 2:48.
12. 2:45.
13. 2:31.
14. 2:7.
15. Hobson, "Playwright Who Always Hid His Pain," p. 35.
16. Ibid.
17. 2:44–45.
18. Geoff Brown, *"The Browning Version," Plays and Players* 23 (March 1976):30.
19. 2:40.
20. Brown, *"The Browning Version,"* p. 30.
21. *New York Times,* 10 October 1948, sec. 11, p. 3, col. 7.
22. Ibid.
23. 2:99.
24. 2:60.
25. 2:66.
26. 2:48.
27. 2:47.
28. Barber, "Obituary."

Chapter Nine

1. 2:xvii.
2. 2:xvi–xvii.
3. Tynan, "Jackpot Rattigan."
4. 2:106.
5. 2:199.

6. 2:115.
7. 2:117.
8. *Times,* 18 March, 1949.
9. Richard Findlater, "The Golden Boy Has Only £5000 to Spend,"
Sunday Dispatch, 14 July 1957.
10. T. C. Worsley, "The Rattigan Version," *New Statesman and Nation,* 26
March 1949, p. 298.
11. Ibid.
12. Philip Oakes, "Grace Before Going," *Sunday Times,* 4 December 1977,
p. 35.
13. 2:xviii.
14. Worsley, "The Rattigan Version," p. 298.
15. 2:115.
16. 2:198.
17. *Times,* 13 June 1961, p. 15, col. c.
18. *New York Times,* 19 March 1949, p. 11, col. 2.
19. Ibid.
20. Ibid.
21. *Times,* 25 October 1950, p. 6, col. e.
22. *New York Times,* 25 October 1950, p. 45, col. 7.
23. 2:xvi.
24. 2:xviii.
25. 2:260.
26. *Times,* 25 October 1950, p. 6, col. e.
27. 2:202.

Chapter Ten

1. T. C. Worsley, "The Expense of Spirit," *New Statesman and Nation,* 15
March 1952, p. 301.
2. Kenneth Tynan, "Jackpot Rattigan."
3. Michael Billington, "The Deep Blue Sea," *Times,* 7 July 1971, p. 7,
col. g.
4. Ibid.
5. David Self, *"Cause Célèbre"* and *"The Deep Blue Sea,"* *Plays and Players,*
September 1977, p.31.
6. 2:336.
7. 2:337.
8. 2:338.
9. 2:313.
10. Simon, "Rattigan Talks," p. 24.
11. 2:361–62.
12. 2:364.
13. 2:365.

14. Simon, "Rattigan Talks," p. 73.
15. Billington, *The Deep Blue Sea,*" p. 7, col. g.
16. 3:94.
17. Logan Gourlay, ed., *Olivier* (New York: Stein and Day, 1974), p. 135.
18. W. A. Darlington, review of *The Sleeping Prince* in *New York Times,* 20 December 1953, sec. 11, p. 4, col. 1.
19. 3:130.
20. Ibid.
21. 3:132.
22. Ibid.
23. Ibid.
24. 3:133.
25. 3:147.
26. 3:150.
27. 3:181.
28. 3:188.
29. 3:182.
30. 3:185.
31. Brooks Atkinson, review of *Separate Tables* in *New York Times,* 26 October 1956, p. 33, col. 1.

Chapter Eleven

1. Barber, "Obituary."
2. 3:305.
3. 3:267.
4. 3:271.
5. 3:271–72.
6. 3:223.
7. John McClain, "Gripping Hit," *Journal American,* 27 December 1961.
8. John Chapman, "John Mills Triumphs," *Daily News,* 27 December 1961.
9. Robert Coleman, "'Ross' Magnificent Study of a Legend," *New York Mirror,* 27 December 1961.
10. Howard Taubman, review of *Ross* in *New York Times,* 7 January 1962, sec. 11, p. 1, col. 1.
11. 3:368.
12. 3:377.
13. 3:386.
14. 3:415.
15. 3:413.
16. 3:418.
17. 4:97.
18. 4:100.

19. Ibid.
20. 4:105.
21. 4:59.
22. Darlow and Hodson, *Terence Rattigan*, p. 271.
23. Bernard Levin, *"Man and Boy,"* *Daily Mail*, 5 September 1963.
24. 4:104.
25. 4:70.
26. Taylor, *Rise and Fall*, p. 144.
27. Ibid., p. 159.
28. Ibid.

Chapter Twelve

1. *Evening Standard*, 6 September 1968.
2. Brigid Brophy, review of *The V.I.P.s* in *New Statesman and Nation*, 20 September 1963.
3. *Evening Standard*, 6 September 1968.
4. Ibid.
5. Ibid.
6. Terence Rattigan, "Why Is Entertainment a Dirty Word?" *Daily Mail*, 2 September 1963.
7. Ibid.
8. "Facts and a Few Figures," notice released by production company, from British Film Institute.
9. Kenneth Tynan, review of *The Yellow Rolls-Royce* in *Observer*, 3 January 1965.
10. Derek Hill, *"The Yellow Rolls-Royce,"* *Sunday Telegraph*, 3 January 1965.
11. Darlow and Hodson, *Terence Rattigan*, p. 75.
12. Ibid.
13. Bosley Crowther, review of *Johnny in the Clouds* in *New York Times*, 16 November 1945, p. 16, col. 2.
14. Bosley Crowther, review of *Breaking Through the Sound Barrier*, in *New York Times*, 7 November 1952, p. 19, col. 1.
15. William Whitebait, *"The Sound Barrier,"* *New Statesman and Nation*, 2 August 1952.
16. *New York Times*, 29 December 1942, p. 27, col. 4.
17. *Times*, 31 July 1951, p. 8, col. d.
18. Hyams, "A Chat," pp. 21–22.
19. Ibid.
20. Philip Oakes, "Living for the Present," *Sunday Times*, 1 February 1976, p. 35.
21. Louise Sweeney, "Make It English Mustard, Please," *Christian Science Monitor*, 29 November 1969.

Chapter Thirteen

1. 4:188.
2. 4:189.
3. 4:214.
4. 4:159.
5. 4:195.
6. 4:218.
7. Sheridan Morley, review of *In Praise of Love, Plays and Players,* November 1973, p. 48.
8. 4:293.
9. 4:242.
10. Morley, review of *In Praise of Love,* p. 49.
11. 4:437.
12. 4:424.
13. 4:428.
14. 4:436–37.
15. 4:436.
16. Ibid.

Chapter Fourteen

1. Mel Gussow, "Stoppard Set to Music," *New York Times,* 29 July 1979, sec. D, p. 22.
2. Hilary Spurling, "Boos from the Stalls," *Observer,* 15 July 1979.

Selected Bibliography

PRIMARY SOURCES

1. Published Plays
The plays of Terence Rattigan are published by Hamish Hamilton of London. Acting editions by Samuel French and Evans Drama Library of London, as well as by Samuel French of New York, are available.

The Collected Plays of Terence Rattigan. London: Hamish Hamilton. Vols. 1 and 2, 1953; vol. 3, 1964; vol. 4, 1978.

Volume 1: *French Without Tears, Flare Path, While the Sun Shines, Love in Idleness, The Winslow Boy.*

Volume 2: *The Browning Version, Harlequinade, Adventure Story, Who Is Sylvia?, The Deep Blue Sea.*

Volume 3: *The Sleeping Prince, Separate Tables, Variation on a Theme, Ross, Heart to Heart,* (a television drama, the only nonstage play included in *Collected Plays*).

Volume 4: *Man and Boy, A Bequest to the Nation, In Praise of Love* (with a curtain-raiser, *Before Dawn*), *Cause Célèbre.*

Individual Publications
Adventure Story. London: Hamish Hamilton, 1950.
After the Dance. London: Hamish Hamilton. 1939.
———. In: *Six Plays of 1939.* London: Hamish Hamilton, 1939.
The Browning Version. In *Three Modern Plays.* London: Methuen, 1958.
Cause Célèbre. London: Hamish Hamilton, 1978.
The Deep Blue Sea. London: Hamish Hamilton, 1952.
———. London: British Book Centre, 1953.
———. New York: Random House, 1952. First American edition inscribed by author.
The Deep Blue Sea with Three Other Plays: Harlequinade, Adventure Story, The Browning Version. London: Pan Books Ltd., 1955.
Flare Path. London: Hamish Hamilton, 1942.
French Without Tears. London: Hamish Hamilton, 1937.
———. New York and Toronto: Farrar and Rinehart, 1938.

162

In Praise of Love. London: Hamish Hamilton, 1973.
Love in Idleness. London: Hamish Hamilton, 1945.
Man and Boy. London: Hamish Hamilton, 1964.
―――. Don Mills, Ontario: Collins, 1964.
O Mistress Mine (American title of *Love in Idleness.*) In *The Best Plays of 1945–46.*
    New York: Edited by Burns Mantle. 1946, pp. 201–34.
Playbill. London: Hamish Hamilton, 1949. *The Browning Version* and *Har-
    lequinade.*
Ross. London: Hamish Hamilton, 1960.
―――. Don Mills, Ontario: Collins, 1960.
―――. New York: Random House, 1962.
Separate Tables. London: Hamish Hamilton, 1955.
―――. New York: Random House, 1955.
―――. New York: Signet Book, 1955.
The Sleeping Prince. London: Hamish Hamilton, 1954.
―――. New York: Random House, 1954.
Variation on a Theme. London: Hamish Hamilton, 1958.
―――. Don Mills, Ontario: Collins, 1960.
While the Sun Shines. London: Hamish Hamilton, 1944.
Who Is Sylvia? London: Hamish Hamilton, 1951.
The Winslow Boy. London: Hamish Hamilton, 1946.
―――. New York: Macmillan, 1962.
―――. London: Hamish Hamilton, 1966. With commentary and notes by
    Keith Nettle.
The Winslow Boy with Two Other Plays: French Without Tears and *Flare Path.*
    London: Pan Books Ltd., 1950.

2. Unpublished plays
First Episode. In collaboration with Philip Heimann.
Follow My Leader. In collaboration with Anthony Maurice.
Grey Farm. In collaboration with Hector Bolitho, adapted from a novel by
    Bolitho.
A Tale of Two Cities. In collaboration with John Gielgud.
Also unpublished are Rattigan's many film scripts and television and radio
    plays, such as *The Final Test, All on Her Own,* and *Nijinsky.*

3. Articles
"An Appreciation of His Work in the Theatre." In *Theatrical Companion to Noel
    Coward.* Edited by Raymond Mander and Joe Mitchenson. London: Max
    Parrish, 1950.
"Concerning the Play of Ideas." *New Statesman and Nation,* 4 March 1950, pp.
    241–42.
"Drama Without Tears." *Times,* 10 October 1937.

Foreword to *I Swore I Never Would*. Harold French. London: Secker & Warburg, 1970.
"A Magnificent Pity for Camels." *Diversion*. Edited by John Sutro. London: Max Parrish, 1950.
"Marilyn, Sir Laurence and I." *Daily Express*, 25 June 1957.
"Mr. Anatole de Grunwald." A tribute. *Times*, 21 January 1967, p. 10.
Noel. Charles Castle. Garden City: Doubleday, 1973. A short contribution by Terence Rattigan.
Olivier. Edited by Logan Gourlay. London: Weidenfelt & Nicholson, 1973. Terence Rattigan contributes a lavish tribute to Sir Laurence Olivier on his performance in *The Sleeping Prince*.
"Personal Tribute, Lieutenant Goldsmith." *Times*, 19 May 1943.
"The Play of Ideas." *New Statesman and Nation*, 13 May 1950, pp. 545–46.
Prefaces to *Collected Plays*. London: Hamish Hamilton, 1953 (vols. 1 and 2); 1964 (vol. 3).
"What Audiences Want to See." *Times*, 27 August 1964, p. 11.
"Why Is Entertainment a Dirty Word?" *Daily Mail*, 2 September 1963.

4. Interviews
Barber, John. "Rattigan's Return." *Daily Telegraph*, 30 July 1973.
Beebe, Lucius. "Playwright Denies the Old School Tie Influences Him." *New York Herald Tribune*, 6 November 1949.
Coleman, Terry. "The Claridges Version." *Guardian*, 20 August 1970.
Curtis, Anthony. "Rattigan's Theatre," BBC Radio 3 program, 30 March 1976.
Edwards, Sydney. *Evening Standard*, 25 November 1969.
Evans, Peter. *Daily Express*, 8 July 1963.
Findlater, Richard. *Sunday Dispatch*, 14 July 1957.
Franklin, Olga. *Daily Mail*, 28 November 1958.
Grosvenor, Peter. *Sunday Express*, 15 November 1968.
Harford, Margaret. "Terence Rattigan Sees the Fadeout of New Theatre." *Los Angeles Times*, 20 November 1969, sec. IV, p. 16.
Hayman, Ronald. "Life for Father." *Times*, 19 September 1970, p. 19.
Hill, Holly. Unpublished interview. New York, 5 December 1974.
Hyams, Barry. "A Chat with Terence Rattigan." *Theatre Arts* 40 (November 1956): 20–22.
Kirkley, Donald. "On Atlantic Voyage." *Chicago Sun*, 8 May 1959.
Lambert, J. W. "Why Rattigan Must Struggle to See His Own Plays." *Sunday Times*, 3 July 1977, p. 5.
Lewis, Emory. "Busy Briton on Broadway." *Cue*, 27 October 1956.
Matthews, Geoffrey. "The Winsome Boy of Sixty." *Evening News*, 10 June 1971.
Morley, Sheridan. "Terence Rattigan at 65." *Times*, 9 May 1977.

————. "The Rattigan Version of His Way to the Stars." Kaleidoscope, Radio 4. *Listener* 18 (August 1977).

Muller, Robert. "Soul-Searching with Terence Rattigan." *Daily Mail,* 30 April 1960.

Oakes, Philip. "Grace Before Going." *Sunday Times,* 4 December 1977, p. 35.

————. "Living for the Present." *Sunday Times,* 1 February 1976.

Pugh, Marshall. "Now That the Shadow Has Passed." *Daily Mail,* 10 December 1964.

Simon, John. "Rattigan Talks to John Simon." *Theatre Arts,* 46 (April 1963):23–24, 73.

Smith, Sydney. "This Pill-Crazy Life Is Not for Me." Interview in Paris, 1956.

Walker, Alexander. "Rattigan on 'My Disastrous Image.'" *Evening Standard,* 23 October 1963.

Watts, Stephen. "Rattigan's Image." *New York Times,* 20 May 1963.

SECONDARY SOURCES

1. Books about Terence Rattigan

Darlow, Michael, and Hodson, Gillian. *Terence Rattigan: The Man and His Work.* London: Quartet, 1979. A fascinating narration of the closeness of Terence Rattigan's plays to his personal life.

Hill, Holly. "A Critical Analysis of the Plays of Terence Rattigan." Ph.D. Diss., City University of New York, 1977. An encyclopedic and indispensable source of information about Terence Rattigan's plays, productions, reviews, and interviews from his earliest juvenilia to *In Praise of Love.*

2. Books about British Theater and Terence Rattigan

Beaton, Cecil. *Memoirs of the 40's.* New York: McGraw Hill, 1970.

Elsom, John. *Post-War British Theatre.* London: Routledge and Kegan Paul, 1976.

Forbes, Bryan. *Dame Edith Evans: Ned's Girl.* Boston: Little, Brown, 1977.

Hayman, Ronald. *British Theatre Since 1955, A Reassessment.* Oxford: Oxford University Press, 1979.

Hinchliffe, Arnold P. *British Theatre, 1950–1970.* Totowa, N.J.: Rowman and Littlefield, 1974.

Lumley, Frederick. *New Trends in Twentieth Century Drama.* New York: Oxford University Press, 1967, pp. 306–10.

Morley, Sheridan. *Review Copies.* Totowa, N.J.: Rowman and Littlefield, 1974.

Taylor, John Russell, *The Rise and Fall of the Well Made Play.* New York: Hill and Wang, 1967.

Trewin, J. C. *Drama in Britain, 1951–1964*. London: Longmans, Green, 1965.
Ustinov, Peter. *Dear Me*. Boston: Little, Brown, 1977.
West, E. J. *Shaw on Theatre*. New York: Hill and Wang, 1958.

3. Articles

Barber, John. *Daily Telegraph*, 1 December 1977. Obituary.
Billington, Michael. "Terence Rattigan." *Guardian*, 2 December 1977. Obituary.
Bolitho, Hector. "Victory Over Cleverness." *Town and Country*, March 1948.
Bridie, James. "The Play of Ideas." *New Statesman and Nation*, 11 March 1950, p. 471.
Brien, Alan. "London Lights Are All Aglow." *Theatre Arts* 45 (February 1961):59–60, 76.
Calta, Louis. "Prolific English Playwright." *New York Times*, 1 December 1977.
Curtis, Anthony. "Professional Man and Boy." *Plays and Players*, February 1978, pp. 21–23.
Drew, Bernard. Interview with Tom Stoppard. "Lifestyle," Westchester–Rockland Newspapers, 20 January 1977, sec. b., p. 2.
Evening Standard, 6 September 1968.
Findlater, Richard. "The Golden Boy Has £5000 to Spend." *Sunday Dispatch*, 14 July 1957.
Foulkes, Richard. "Terence Rattigan's Variations on a Theme." *Modern Drama*, December 1979, pp. 375–81.
Fry, Christopher. "The Play of Ideas." *New Statesman and Nation*, 22 April 1950, p. 458.
Gilder, Rosamund. "Sprightly Entertainment." *Theatre Arts* 30 (March 1946):133.
Gottfried, Martin. "In Praise of Craftsmanship." *Stagebill*, John F. Kennedy Center for the Performing Arts, November 1974.
Gussow, Mel. "Stoppard Set to Music." *New York Times*, 29 July 1979, p. 22.
Hall, Fernell. "The Play of Ideas." *New Statesman and Nation*, 18 March 1950, p. 301.
Hast, Norman. "Introducing Terence Rattigan." *Theatre World*, April 1939, p. 180.
Hobson, Harold. "The Playwright Who Always Hid His Pain." *Sunday Times*, 4 December 1977.
Home, William Douglas. "Terence Rattigan Remembered." *Times*, 10 February 1978. A tribute read by Donald Sinden at memorial service at St. Martin-in-the-Fields.
Levy, Benn Wolfe. "The Play of Ideas." *New Statesman and Nation*, 25 March 1978, p. 338.

Marshall, Arthur. "Without Tears." *New Statesman and Nation,* 9 December 1977, p. 813.

Marvell, Roger. "Flare Path." *New Statesman and Nation,* 22 August 1942, p. 124.

Oakes, Philip. "Grace Before Going." *Sunday Times,* 4 December 1977, p. 35.

O'Casey, Sean. "The Play of Ideas." *New Statesman and Nation,* 8 April 1950, pp. 397–98.

"Out Goes Absurdism—in Comes the New Naturalism." *New York Times,* 19 March 1978, sec. 2, p. 1.

Scott-Kilvert, Ian. "The Play of Ideas." *New Statesman and Nation,* 29 April 1950, p. 486.

Shaw, George Bernard. "The Play of Ideas." *New Statesman and Nation,* 6 May 1950, pp. 426–27.

"Sir Terence Rattigan, Enduring Influence on the English Theatre." *Times,* 1 December 1977, p. 16. Obituary.

Smith, Kay Nolte. "Terence Rattigan." *Objectivist,* March 1971, pp. 9–15.

Spurling, Hilary. "Boos from the Stalls." *Observer,* 15 July 1979.

Sweeney, Louise, "Make It English Mustard, Please." *Christian Science Monitor,* 29 November 1969.

Tynan, Kenneth. "Jackpot Rattigan." *Evening Standard,* 1 July 1953.

Ustinov, Peter. "The Play of Ideas." *New Statesman and Nation,* 1 April 1950, p. 367.

Willis, Ted. "The Play of Ideas." *New Statesman and Nation,* 15 April 1950, pp. 426–27.

Worsley, T. C. "The Expense of Spirit." *New Statesman and Nation,* 15 March 1952, p. 301.

———. "Rattigan and His Critics." *London Magazine* 4, n.s. 6 (September 1964):60–72.

4. Reviews

"Adventure Story." *Times,* 18 March 1949.

———. *New York Times,* 19 March 1949, p. 11.

———. *Times,* 13 June 1961, p. 15.

"After the Dance." *Times,* 22 June 1939, p. 14.

———. *New Statesman and Nation,* 1 July 1939, p. 14.

———. *New York Times,* 16 July 1939, p. 2.

Atkinson, Brooks. *"Separate Tables."* *New York Times,* 26 October 1956, p. 33.

Barber, John. *"Cause Célèbre."* *Daily Telegraph,* 1 December 1977.

Billington, Michael. *"The Deep Blue Sea."* *Times* 7 July 1971, p. 7.

Brophy, Brigid. *"Man and Boy."* *New Statesman and Nation,* 20 September 1963.

Brown, Geoff. *"The Browning Version."* *Plays and Players* 23 (March 1976):35.

"The Browning Version." *New York Times,* 7 March 1958, p. 17.

Chapman, John. *"Ross."* Daily News, 27 December 1961.
Coleman, Robert. *"Ross."* New York Mirror, 27 December 1961.
Crowther, Bosley. *"Breaking Through the Sound Barrier."* New York Times, 7 November 1952, p. 19.
————. *"Johnny in the Clouds."* New York Times, 16 November 1945.
Darlington, W. A. *"Flare Path."* New York Times, 23 August 1942, p. 1.
————. *"The Sleeping Prince."* New York Times, 20 December 1953, p. 4.
"The Final Test." New York Times, 31 July 1951, p. 8.
"First Episode." Times, 27 January 1934.
————. New York Times, 13 September 1934, p. 18.
"Follow My Leader." Times, 17 January 1940, p. 6.
————. New Statesman and Nation, 27 January 1940.
"French without Tears." New York Times, 19 March 1974, p. 28.
Gottfried, Martin. *"In Praise of Love."* New York Post, 11 December 1974.
"Heart to Heart." Times, 7 December 1962, p. 8.
Hill, Derek. *"The Yellow Rolls-Royce."* Sunday Telegraph, 3 January 1965.
"Joie de Vivre." Times, 15 July 1960, p. 16.
Levin, Bernard. *"Man and Boy."* Daily Mail, 5 September 1963.
"Love in Idleness." New Statesman and Nation, 30 December 1944.
————. New York Times, 7 January 1945, p. 2.
————. New York Times, 1 September 1946, p. 1.
McClain, John. *"Ross."* Journal American, 27 December 1961.
Marvell, Roger. *"Flare Path."* New Statesman and Nation, 22 August 1942, p. 124.
Matthews, Geoffrey. "The Winsome Boy of Sixty." Evening News, 10 June 1971.
Morley, Sheridan. *"In Praise of Love."* Plays and Players 20 (November 1973):48–49.
Nichols, Lewis. *"Flare Path."* New York Times, 24 December 1942, p. 20.
————. *"While the Sun Shines."* New York Times, 20 September 1944, p. 21.
"Playbill." New York Times, 10 October 1948, p. 3.
Self, David. *"Cause Célèbre"/"The Deep Blue Sea,"* Plays and Players, September 1977, pp. 30–31.
Taubman, Howard. *"Ross."* New York Times, 7 January 1962, sec. 2, p. 1.
Tynan, Kenneth. *"The Yellow Rolls-Royce."* Observer, 3 January 1965.
Whitebait, William. *"The Sound Barrier."* New Statesman and Nation, 2 August 1952.
"Who Is Sylvia?" New York Times, 25 October 1950, p. 45.
————. Times, 25 October 1950, p. 6.
Worsley, T. C. *"Adventure Story."* New Statesman and Nation, 26 March 1949, p. 298.

Index